knitting *little luxuries*

knitting *little luxuries*

LOUISA HARDING

INTERWEAVE PRESS

Photography, Stephen Jessup
Cover and interior design, Karla Baker
Technical editor, Karen Frisa

Text © 2007 Louisa Harding
Photography © Stephen Jessup
Illustrations © Interweave Press LLC

INTERWEAVE PRESS.
interweavebooks.com

Interweave Press LLC
201 East Fourth Street
Loveland, CO 80537-5655 USA
interweavebooks.com

Printed in China by Asia Pacific Offset.

Library of Congress Cataloging-in-Pub-
lication Data

Harding, Louisa.
  Knitting little luxuries : beautiful acces-
sories to knit / Louisa Harding.
      p. cm.
  Includes index.
  ISBN 978-1-59668-054-8
  1. Knitting. 2. Knitting--Patterns. I.
Title.
  TT820.H266 2007
  746.43'2041--dc22

2007018444

10 9 8 7 6 5 4 3 2 1

ACKNOWLEDGMENTS

This book is dedicated to three very important women in my life: my grandmother Dorothy, who taught me to knit and whose button box I still use; my mother, Daphne, from whom I inherited my love of all things girly; and my stepmother, Dianne, who encouraged my love of fabric and sewing. The combined influence and never ending support from these three wonderful women has defined the woman and designer I am. Thank you.

As always, I thank Stephen Jessup for wonderful photographs and for being my rock, and our children, Belle and Oscar. Thankfully, children change everything.

This book would not be possible without the help of my wonderful knitters Betty Rothwell, Mrs. Marsh, Daphne Harding, Mary Butler, Mrs. Wilmot, and Janet Mann. I would like to thank the models, Cecily Alder and Alicia Pollett, as well as Michael Richmond for being such a wonderfully creative makeup and hair artist, and Andy Richards, our photographer's assistant.

Thank you to Marilyn Phillips at the Battery. The look of this book was greatly enhanced by the wonderful location at which we took the photographs. Marilyn is an inspiration to creative women everywhere. Thank you also to Deb Price (debpricejewellery.co.uk) for the jewelry pieces commissioned to enhance and reflect the knitted pieces.

Finally, thank you to Anne Merrow, my wonderful editor, who thankfully turns my written waffle into readable coherent text, and Tricia Waddell and the fantastic team of women at Interweave Press for their support, understanding, and encouragement, which enabled this exciting book to happen.

CONTENTS

KNITTING WOMEN

Knitting Little Luxuries is a book of simple, beautiful, and quick-to-knit projects that are perfect to make as gifts for friends or to indulge yourself. The projects are unashamedly feminine and have been designed to unleash creative talents and excite an appreciation of wonderful yarns as well as the craft of knitting.

Women who knit have a kinship with fellow knitters, getting together at each others' houses or the local yarn store to be enveloped by yarn, needles, notions, and patterns, immersing themselves in color and texture. In these surroundings, supported and nurtured by like-minded women, knitters are able to unleash a creativity that is not always obvious in ordinary daily life, sharing knowledge and practical skills as well as an appreciation of fiber and yarn. In this shared creative pursuit women find a sisterhood, a common thread, a support that goes far beyond the knitting, quite often knitting themselves into each others' lives. This book is dedicated to and inspired by women, especially my grandmother Dorothy Louisa, after whom I was named and from whom I learned to knit.

INHERITING OUR CRAFT

When my grandmother died I inherited her sewing basket and button tin. Opening her sewing basket was like opening a treasure chest, not just of sewing and knitting notions but also of childhood memories of sitting at her knee watching her sew or knit and listening to stories of her life. I remember many happy hours sorting all these buttons by colors, sizes, and shapes. My own children now do the same, threading buttons onto strings and making bracelets and necklaces. I take great pleasure in the fact that even today my children enjoy the simple delight offered by my grandmother's button box on a rainy afternoon.

My grandmother grew up in very different times, born in 1911 as the second child in a family of seven. For her, making things for the home and to wear was

a matter of necessity. Women of my grandmother's generation inherited their craft skills from sitting with their grandmothers, mothers, and aunts as they passed on skills that have not changed in centuries. Through this book I have the privilege of sharing the knowledge passed down to me with others.

Because making things was a necessity for my grandmother's generation, they had to be very inventive. As materials were scarce, they were the originators of recycling. Dorothy would reuse old fabrics, unravel old sweaters, and take buttons from worn-out clothes, then turn them into something new and unique.

WOMEN UNIQUE

The idea of uniqueness was my initial inspiration for the projects in this book. I wanted to design pieces that were very easy and simple to knit, which could be made unique by the addition of found objects, buttons, flowers, ribbons, and embellishment with embroidery, making every piece as individual as the women

knitting them. The buttons and ribbons that I used as embellishment came from Dorothy's sewing basket and button tin.

Using the women in my life as inspiration, I wanted the chapters in this book to reflect the different sides of women. There are many variations within female taste—we may not all like girly pink, but we can appreciate that a friend or relative may love it. With this in mind, the chapters and projects in this book have been designed to appeal to our different personalities.

I know that Dorothy would be amazed at the sumptuous fibers and the wide range of yarns available today. She would be astonished by the spectrum of colors and textures and the wide variety of patterns. My sincerest hope is that through my books I am able to pass on the handicraft knowledge I learned from her to my daughter, my nieces, and friends. My hope is that through knitting, sharing, and giving the projects in this book, you too will pass on your wisdom and keep the appreciation of these craft skills alive for generations of women in the future.

WHAT DO YOU FEEL LIKE KNITTING TODAY?

eclectic and quirky

This chapter uses embellishment, stitch structures, and yarn combinations to show how different styles can be mixed. With the addition of vintage trimmings and buttons, each project becomes a unique piece reflecting the knitter or gift recipient.

textured and modern

I wanted to reflect a modern woman in this chapter by using cables and interesting stitch fabrics. These pieces turn conventional knitting techniques upside down by experimenting with offbeat constructions.

pretty and feminine

Using color, texture, and lace stitches, the projects in this chapter have a distinctly girly theme. The pieces use luxury fibers such as silk/wool blends, angora, and pretty ribbons. These are designs that capture and embrace the glamorous side of women, the little things that make us feel special from the inside.

traditional and folk

Traditional Fair Isle stitch patterns in the projects in this chapter establish the old-fashioned ambience of warmth and comfort, but with a modern twist.

eclectic + QUIRKY

Embrace embellishment to make your knitting one of a kind. Pair simple knitting techniques with embroidery, ribbon, and buttons to create projects reminiscent of a past age, when dexterity and individuality were commonplace, and time was not so scarce.

Although many of the projects in this chapter are simple to knit, they become unique with the addition of embellishment. Knit these beautiful pieces in wonderful yarns, then take the time to make each piece truly individual. With the addition of vintage trimmings and buttons, each project reflects the knitter and the recipient, creating an heirloom of the future.

cecily
BEANIE

This basic hat can be knitted very quickly, and then it becomes a blank canvas for unleashing creative ideas. For a girly feel, embellish the hat with buttons and flowers; alternatively, add dramatic pom-poms. Let your imagination take hold—scour the bottom of your sewing basket or knitting stash, knit stripes, add lazy daisies, sew on beads… Make this hat as individual as you dare.

FINISHED MEASUREMENTS

20¼" (51.5 cm) circumference, to fit an average female head.

YARN

Worsted weight (#4 Medium).

SHOWN HERE

Louisa Harding Kashmir Aran (55% merino wool, 10% cashmere, 35% microfiber; 83 yd [76 m]/50 g):
beanie with pom-poms (page 17): #2 sky (blue, MC), 2 balls, and #6 lime (for pom-poms), 1 ball.
embellished beanie (opposite): #14 biscuit (tan, MC), 2 balls.

NEEDLES

U.S. size 6 (4 mm) and U.S. size 7 (4.5 mm). Adjust needle size if necessary to obtain the correct gauge.

NOTIONS

both hats: Tapestry needle.
pom-pom beanie only: Size G/6 (4 mm) crochet hook.
embellished beanie only: Sewing needle and thread; about 40 mother-of-pearl buttons; about 12 small fabric flowers; small flower bouquet; 12" (30.5 cm) length of ¼" (6 mm) ribbon.

GAUGE

18 sts and 27 rows = 4" (10 cm) in St st on larger needles.

BEANIE

EDGING

With MC and smaller needles, CO 91 sts. Work 6 rows in St st, then work 2 rows in garter st.

Change to larger needles and work in St st until piece measures 5" (12.5 cm) from CO (4" [10 cm] when edge is allowed to roll), ending with a WS row.

CROWN

ROW 1: (RS) [K7, k2tog] 10 times, k1—81 sts rem.

ROW 2 AND EVERY WS ROW: Purl.

ROW 3: [K6, k2tog] 10 times, k1—71 sts rem.

ROW 5: [K5, k2tog] 10 times, k1—61 sts rem.

ROW 7: [K4, k2tog] 10 times, k1—51 sts rem.

ROW 9: [K3, k2tog] 10 times, k1—41 sts rem.

ROW 11: [K2, k2tog] 10 times, k1—31 sts rem.

ROW 13: [K1, k2tog] 10 times, k1—21 sts rem.

ROW 15: [K2tog] 10 times, k1—11 sts rem.

Break yarn, leaving a 12" (30.5 cm) tail. Thread tail through rem sts, pull tight to gather sts, and fasten off inside.

With MC threaded on a tapestry needle and beg at gathered top, sew seam using mattress stitch or backstitch (see Glossary, page 124), reversing seam for lower ¾" (2 cm) for rolled brim.

FINISHING

BEANIE WITH POM-POMS

With lime, make four 1" (2.5 cm) pom-poms and four 1½" (3.8 cm) pom-poms (see Glossary, page 121). Attach 3 of the smaller pom-poms and 2 of the larger pom-poms to hat using crochet chains as foll: with crochet hook, join lime to hat and crochet a chain (see Glossary, page 118) 1–3" (2.5–7.5 cm) long. Fasten off, leaving a 6" (15 cm) tail. Attach pom-pom to tail. Sew rem 3 pom-poms directly to hat, arranging as shown above.

EMBELLISHED BEANIE

With MC threaded on a tapestry needle, sew mother-of-pearl buttons to the hat as shown at left. With sewing needle and thread, sew small fabric flowers to the hat, attaching with small stitches on WS of hat. Tie the length of ribbon around the flower bouquet and secure with a bow, trim ends of ribbon, and sew bouquet into place with small stitches on WS of hat.

daphne
PURSE

This purse was inspired by the wonderful embroidered straw bags popular in the 1950s. The yarn, a blend of linen, silk, and cotton, reminds me of golden straw. The herringbone stitch pattern makes the bag dense like a woven fabric and very strong and hard-wearing. I love the three-dimensional flowers, which bring this piece to life.

FINISHED MEASUREMENTS

About 11¾" (30 cm) wide and 11" (28 cm) long.

YARN

Worsted weight (#4 Medium).

SHOWN HERE

Louisa Harding Cinnabar (30% viscose, 25% cotton, 15% acrylic, 10% silk, 10% linen, 5% polyamid, 5% acetate; 87 yd [80 m]/50 g): #5 raffia, 5 balls.

NEEDLES

U.S. size 5 (3.75 mm) and U.S. size 6 (4 mm). Adjust needle size if necessary to obtain the correct gauge.

NOTIONS

Tapestry needle; assorted lengths of ribbon yarn for flower embroidery; sewing needle and thread; 7 small fabric flowers; 13" x 22" (33 cm x 56 cm) fabric (for lining); 12" x 19" (30.5 cm x 48.5 cm) iron-on interfacing (for body of purse); two 12" x 2" (30.5 cm x 5 cm) pieces iron-on interfacing (for handles); pins; iron.

GAUGE

27 sts and 48 rows = 4" (10 cm) in herringbone st on larger needles.

STITCH GUIDE

HERRINGBONE STITCH:

ROW 1: (RS) K3, [sl 2 with yarn in front (wyf), k2] 19 times, k1.

ROW 2: K1, p1, [sl 2 with yarn in back (wyb), p2] 19 times, p1, k1.

ROW 3: K1, [sl 2 wyf, k2] 19 times, sl 2 wyf, k1.

ROW 4: K1, p3, [sl 2 wyb, p2] 18 times, sl 2 wyb, p1, k1.

ROWS 5-12: Rep Rows 1–4 twice more.

ROW 13: K1, [sl 2 wyf, k2] 19 times, sl 2 wyf, k1.

ROW 14: K1, p1, [sl 2 wyb, p2] 19 times, p1, k1.

ROW 15: K3, [sl 2 wyf, k2] 19 times, k1.

ROW 16: K1, p3, [sl 2 wyb, p2] 18 times, sl 2 wyb, p1, k1.

ROWS 17-24: Rep Rows 13–16 twice more.

Rep Rows 1–24 for patt.

PURSE

FIRST SIDE

With smaller needles, CO 70 sts. Work 3 rows in garter st.

NEXT ROW: (WS; inc row) [K4, M1 (see Glossary, page 122), k3] 10 times—80 sts.

Change to larger needles and work 16 rows in herringbone st (see Stitch Guide).

FIRST HANDLE

ROW 1: (RS) K1, [sl 2 wyf, k2] 6 times, k32, [sl 2 wyf, k2] 5 times, sl 2 wyf, k1.

ROW 2: (WS) K1, p1, [sl 2 wyb, p2] 5 times, sl 2 wyb, p1, BO 30 sts knitwise (24 sts rem on left needle), p2, [sl 2 wyb, p2] 5 times, p1, k1.

ROW 3: K3, [sl 2 wyf, k2] 5 times, k2, turn, CO 30 sts using the cable method (see Glossary, page 117), turn, k4, [sl 2 wyf, k2] 5 times, k1.

ROW 4: K1, p3, [sl 2 wyb, p2] 5 times, p1, k30, p1, [sl 2 wyb, p2] 5 times, sl 2 wyb, p1, k1.
Work Rows 13–16 of herringbone st.

BODY

Work Rows 1–24 of herringbone st 4 times, then work Rows 1–12 once more—piece measures about 11½" (29 cm) from CO.

FOLD LINE

Work 2 rows in garter st.

SECOND SIDE

Work Rows 1–24 of herringbone st 4 times, then work Rows 1–16 once more—piece measures about 21¼" (54 cm) from CO.

SECOND HANDLE

Rep Rows 1–4 of first handle. Work Rows 13–16 of herringbone st once, then work Rows 1–12 once.

NEXT ROW: (RS; dec row) [K4, k2tog, k2] 10 times—70 sts rem.

Work 3 rows in garter st.

BO all sts.

FINISHING

Block purse according to yarn care instructions. With ribbon yarn threaded on a tapestry needle, embroider groups of 5-petal lazy daisies (see Glossary, page 120) on first side of purse as shown at opposite. Join groups of lazy daisies with running stitch (see Glossary, page 120) to create stalks, and add French knots (see Glossary, page 120) as desired. Using sewing needle and thread, sew fabric flowers into place and secure with small stitches on WS of purse.

HANDLES

With purse laid flat and WS facing, place interfacing for handles above handle opening (between opening and CO or BO edge, as shown at right) and iron in place.

Fold top of purse so that CO edge meets top of handle opening and, with yarn threaded on a tapestry needle, whipstitch into place. Whipstitch ends of handles together neatly on RS. Repeat for BO edge.

PURSE BODY

With WS of purse facing, place interfacing for body between handle openings and iron in place.

Fold purse in half at bottom fold line with right sides together. Use backstitch (see Glossary, page 124) to sew side seams. Turn purse RS out.

PURSE LINING

Fold lining fabric in half with right sides together. With sewing needle and thread, sew side seams using backstitch and leaving ½" (1.3 cm) seam allowance.

Slip lining inside purse, turning under a ½" (1.3 cm) seam allowance at top, and pin into place just below handles. Use a short running st to sew lining into place.

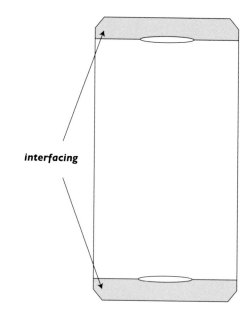

interfacing

elsie MITTENS

These basic mittens are knitted flat and seamed afterwards, making them the ideal canvas for adding embroidered embellishment. The luxurious yarns used for this pattern—a silk and wool blend for the striped mittens and a beautifully soft fluffy angora for the embroidered mittens—will keep fingers toasty all winter.

FINISHED SIZE

6¾" (17 cm) circumference measured above the thumb.

YARN

DK weight (#3 Light).

SHOWN HERE

striped mittens (opposite): Louisa Harding Grace (50% merino wool, 50% silk; 110 yd [101 m]/50 g): #3 dove (gray), #5 olive, and #4 rose, 1 ball each.

embellished mittens (page 28): Louisa Harding Kimono Angora Pure (70% angora, 25% wool, 5% nylon; 125 yd [114 m]/25 g): #1 rice (tan), 2 balls; and Louisa Harding Thalia (52% polyamid, 24% acrylic, 12% mohair, 6% wool, 6% metallic; 93 yd [85 m]/50 g): #1 natural (brown/gray multi), 1 hank.

NEEDLES

U.S. size 3 (3.25 mm), U.S. size 6 (4 mm), and U.S. size 8 (5 mm). Adjust needle size if necessary to obtain the correct gauge.

NOTIONS

Markers (m); tapestry needle.

GAUGE

22 sts and 30 rows = 4" (10 cm) in St st with Grace or Kimono Angora Pure on middle-size needles.

STITCH GUIDE

STRIPED STOCKINETTE STITCH:

ROW 1: Olive.

ROWS 2 AND 3: Rose.

ROW 4: Olive.

ROWS 5–8: Gray.

Rep Rows 1–8 for patt.

STRIPED MITTENS

RIGHT HAND

Cuff

With olive and largest needles, CO 57 sts.

Change to rose and middle-size needles; knit 1 row.

NEXT ROW: (WS; dec row) *P1, p2tog; rep from * to end—38 sts rem.

Change to gray and smallest needles; knit 1 row.

RIB ROW 1: (WS) *P2, k2; rep from * to last 2 sts, p2.

RIB ROW 2: (RS) *K2, p2; rep from * to last 2 sts, k2.

Rep Rib Rows 1 and 2 thirteen more times, then rep Row 1 once more—piece measures about 3¾" (9.5 cm).

Change to middle-size needles and, beg with a knit row, work 8 rows in striped St st (see Stitch Guide).

Thumb gusset

Cont in striped St st, shape gusset as foll:

ROW 1: (RS; inc row) K20, place marker (pm), M1 (see Glossary, page 121), k3, M1, pm, k15—40 sts.

Work 3 rows even in striped St st.

INC ROW: K20, sl m, M1, knit to m, M1, sl m, k15—2 sts inc'd.

Rep inc row every 4th row 3 more times—48 sts. Work 1 WS row even.

Divide for thumb

NEXT ROW: (RS) K33, turn.

NEXT ROW: P13. These 13 sts form the thumb.

With gray and beg with a knit row, work 15 rows in St st over 13 thumb sts.

NEXT ROW: (WS; dec row) P1, [p2tog] 6 times—7 sts rem.

Break yarn, run tail through rem thumb sts, pull tight to gather, and fasten off inside. With gray threaded on a tapestry needle, sew thumb seam.

With RS facing and rose, beg at thumb, pick up and knit

2 sts from base of thumb, then knit to end of row—37 sts. Cont in striped St st as established, work 25 rows even.

Shape top

ROW 1: (RS; dec row) K1, [ssk (see Glossary, page 119), k13, k2tog, k1] 2 times—33 sts rem.

ROW 2 AND ALL WS ROWS: Purl.

ROW 3: (dec row) K1, [ssk, k11, k2tog, k1] 2 times—29 sts rem.

ROW 5: K1, [ssk, k9, k2tog, k1] 2 times—25 sts rem.

ROW 7: K1, [ssk, k7, k2tog, k1] 2 times—21 sts rem.

BO all sts.

LEFT HAND

Work as for Right Hand to thumb gusset.

Thumb gusset

Cont in striped St st, shape gusset as foll:

ROW 1: (RS) K15, pm, M1, k3, M1, pm, k20—40 sts. Work 3 rows even.

INC ROW: K15, sl m, M1, knit to m, M1, sl m, k20—2 sts inc'd.

Rep inc row every 4th row 3 more times—48 sts. Work 1 WS row even.

Divide for thumb

NEXT ROW: (RS) K28, turn.

NEXT ROW: P13.

Cont as for right-hand mitten thumb, then work hand and top as for right-hand mitten.

EMBROIDERY

With contrasting yarn threaded on a tapestry needle, embroider on stripes. As shown on page 24, use a combination of French knots, cross-stitch, duplicate stitch, and single lazy daisy loops (see Glossary, page 120). For variety and visual interest, the mittens shown are not identical.

EMBELLISHED MITTENS

RIGHT HAND

With brown/gray multi, largest needles, and leaving an 8" (20.5 cm) tail, CO 57 sts. Break yarn, leaving an 8" (20.5 cm) tail. Change to tan and middle-size needles; knit 1 row.

Beg with dec row, cont as for right-hand striped mitten, working in tan throughout and omitting embroidery.

LEFT HAND

Work as for right-hand embellished mitten to thumb gusset.

Complete as for left-hand striped mitten, working in tan throughout and omitting embroidery.

EMBROIDERY

With brown/gray multi threaded on a tapestry needle, embroider mittens with large 4-petal lazy daisies with French knots in the centers as shown at right.

FINISHING

Sew side seams, using mattress stitch or backstitch (see Glossary, page 124). For embroidered mittens, tie CO tails in bows at wrist.

alice BERET

The soft, chalky pastel stripes of this jaunty tam remind me of 1920s bathing suits and swimming caps, while its shape hints at the cheeky fashions of the Flapper era. The bright picot edge adds light and texture around the face, while a knitted bow stitched on the side completes the delicate but sassy look.

FINISHED SIZE

22" (56 cm) head circumference.

YARN

Worsted weight (#4 Medium).

SHOWN HERE

Louisa Harding Nautical Cotton (100% mercerized cotton; 93 yd [85 m]/50 g): #20 butter (yellow), #23 sage, #21 mauve, #13 beige (brown), #2 natural (cream), and #6 lime, 1 ball each.

NEEDLES

U.S. size 3 (3.25 mm) and U.S. size 5 (3.75 mm). Adjust needle size if necessary to obtain the correct gauge.

NOTIONS

Tapestry needle; sewing needle and thread; 22" (56 cm) length of 1" (2.5 mm) bias binding.

GAUGE

22 sts and 28 rows = 4" (10 cm) in striped St st on larger needles.

NOTE

* Because some people can't wear wool next to the skin, this hat is designed to be knitted in cotton, but cotton yarns have no elasticity. A traditional millinery trick—bias binding sewn inside the brim—makes the hat hold its shape.

STITCH GUIDE
STRIPED ST ST:

ROWS 1 AND 2: Mauve.

ROWS 3 AND 4: Brown.

ROWS 5 AND 6: Cream.

ROWS 7 AND 8: Lime.

ROWS 9 AND 10: Yellow.

ROWS 11 AND 12: Sage.

Rep Rows 1–12 for patt.

HAT

BRIM

With yellow and smaller needles, work picot CO as foll: *CO 5 sts using the cable method (see Glossary, page 117), BO 2 sts, slip st on right needle back to left needle—3 sts CO; rep from * until there are 99 sts on left needle, CO 1 st—100 sts.

Change to sage and work 15 rows in garter st.

DEC ROW: Knit to last 2 sts, k2tog—99 sts rem.

STRIPED SECTION

Change to larger needles and beg striped St st (see Stitch Guide), and at the same time work increases and decreases as foll:

INC ROW: (RS) [K3, M1 (see Glossary, page 122), k4, M1] 14 times, k1—127 sts.

Work 11 rows even in striped St st, ending with a WS row.

INC ROW: (RS) [K9, M1] 14 times, k1—141 sts.

Work 13 rows even in striped St st.

DEC ROW: (RS) [K8, k2tog] 14 times, k1—127 sts rem.

Work 7 rows even in striped St st.

DEC ROW: (RS) [K7, k2tog] 14 times, k1—113 sts rem. Work 3 rows even in striped St st.

DEC ROW: (RS) [K6, k2tog] 14 times, k1—99 sts rem. Work 3 rows even in striped St st.

DEC ROW: (RS) [K5, k2tog] 14 times, k1—85 sts rem. Work 3 rows even in striped St st.

DEC ROW: (RS) [K4, k2tog] 14 times, k1—71 sts rem. Work 1 row even in striped St st.

DEC ROW: (RS) [K3, k2tog] 14 times, k1—57 sts rem. Work 1 row even in striped St st.

DEC ROW: (RS) [K2, k2tog] 14 times, k1—43 sts rem. Work 1 row even in striped St st.

Work next 2 rows using brown.

DEC ROW: (RS) [K1, k2tog] 14 times, k1—29 sts rem.

DEC ROW: (WS) P1, [p2tog] 14 times—15 sts rem.

Break yarn, thread tail through rem sts, pull tight to gather, and fasten off inside.

Sew seam using mattress stitch or backstitch (see Glossary, page 124).

FINISHING

BOW

With smaller needles and sage, CO 20 sts. Work 17 rows in garter st, ending with a RS row. BO all sts knitwise on WS.

CENTER KNOT

With smaller needles and sage, CO 10 sts. Beg with a knit row, work 4 rows in St st. BO all sts. Sew sides of center knot together.

Thread bow through center knot. With sewing needle and thread, attach bow to brim as shown at left.

BRIM

Being sure that bias binding fits around the wearer's head, use needle and thread to sew bias binding to inside of brim.

dottie
WRAP

This simple but quirky knitted wrap is embellished with blanket stitch and buttons. The piece was inspired by odd buttons that I inherited in my grandmother's button box, each one with its own history. Using your own vintage buttons (or beads or brooches) will create a uniquely personal piece to cherish.

FINISHED SIZE

32" (81.5 cm) wide, measured at shoulder, and 14" (35.5 cm) long.

YARN

Worsted weight (#4 Medium).

SHOWN HERE

Louisa Harding Kashmir Aran (55% merino wool, 10% cashmere, 35% microfiber; 83 yd [76 m]/50 g): #3 rose, 6 balls; #19 mustard and #10 purple, 1 ball each; #8 olive, less than 1 ball.

NEEDLES

U.S size 7 (4.5 mm) and U.S. size 8 (5 mm). Adjust needle size if necessary to obtain the correct gauge.

NOTIONS

Tapestry needle; fine-eyed tapestry needle or sewing needle and thread (for sewing on buttons); three ⅞" (2.2 cm) buttons for closure; about 80 buttons of various shapes, sizes, and colors for embellishment.

GAUGE

18 sts and 24 rows = 4" (10 cm) in textured St st on larger needles.

Textured Stockinette Stitch

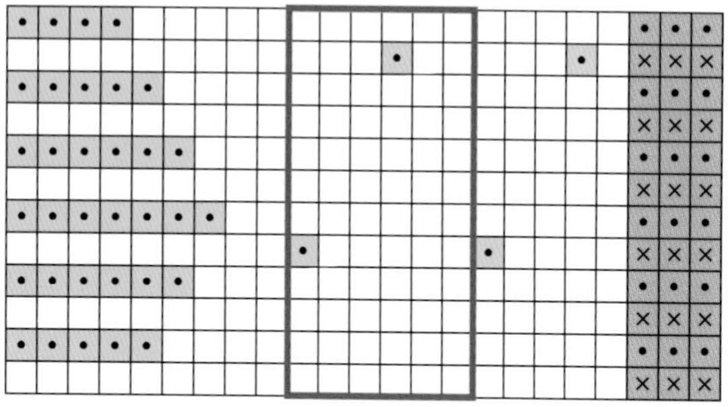

Chart legend:

- ☐ with rose, k on RS, p on WS
- ▪ with rose, p on RS, k on WS
- ☒ with mustard, k on RS, p on WS
- ▪ with mustard, p on RS, k on WS
- ☐ pattern repeat

Row numbers on chart (right side): 11, 9, 7, 5, 3, 1

WRAP

With mustard and smaller needles, CO 53 sts. Work 4 rows in garter st, ending with a WS row.

Change to larger needles and work Textured St st chart until piece measures 38½" (98 cm) from CO, ending with a WS row.

Change to smaller needles. With mustard, work 4 rows in garter st. BO all sts.

SHOULDER EDGING

With purple and smaller needles, CO 10 sts; with RS of wrap facing, pick up and knit 137 sts along left edge of piece—147 sts total. Knit 1 row.

ROW 1: (RS) With mustard, *k1, sl 1 pwise; rep from * to last st, k1.

ROW 2: *K1, sl 1 pwise with yarn in front (wyf); rep from * to last st, k1.

ROWS 3 AND 4: With rose, knit.

ROW 5: With purple, k1, *k1, sl 1 pwise; rep from * to last 2 sts, k2.

ROW 6: K1, *k1, sl 1 pwise wyf; rep from * to last 2 sts, k2.

ROW 7: (buttonhole row) With rose, k3, k2tog, yo, knit to end.

ROW 8: Knit.

ROW 9: With mustard, *k1, sl 1 pwise; rep from * to last st, k1.

ROW 10: *K1, sl 1 pwise wyf; rep from * to last st, k1.

ROWS 11 AND 12: With rose, knit.

ROW 13: (buttonhole row) K3, k2tog, yo, *k1, sl 1 pwise; rep from * to last 2 sts, k2.

ROW 14: K1, *k1, sl 1 pwise wyf; rep from * to last 2 sts, k2.

ROWS 15 AND 16: Knit.

ROW 17: *K1, sl 1 pwise; rep from * to last st, k1.

ROW 18: *K1, sl 1 pwise wyf; rep from * to last st, k1.

ROW 19: (buttonhole row) K3, k2tog, yo, knit to end.

Knit 2 rows. With mustard, knit 2 rows. With purple, knit 2 rows. BO all sts knitwise.

FINISHING

Sew buttons for closure opposite buttonholes. Embellish shoulder edging with buttons arranged randomly, as shown at right.

With purple, define the garter st zigzag by threading the yarn under the last purl st at the edge of the zigzag to outline it.

With olive threaded on a tapestry needle, work blanket stitch (see Glossary, page 119) around all edges.

betty WRAP

This delicate and pretty wrap looks far more intricate and complicated to knit than it really is—the colors and simple lace pattern do all the work, and the yarn is used double for quick knitting. The button closure, placed deliberately askew, gives the piece a flirty asymmetry.

FINISHED SIZE

39½ (44, 49)" (100.5 [112, 124.5] cm) long and 13" (33 cm) wide.

YARN

DK weight (#3 Light) and chunky weight (#5 Bulky).

SHOWN HERE

Louisa Harding Grace (50% merino wool, 50% silk; 110 yd [101 m]/50 g): #4 rose (A), 3 balls, and #13 aqua (C), 2 balls. Louisa Harding Sari Ribbon (90% polyamid, 10% metallic; 66 yd [60 m]/50 g): #23 bon bon (pink/blue/green, B), 1 hank. Louisa Harding Impressions (16% kid mohair, 84% polyamid; 154 yd [141 m]/50 g): #14 fanfare (pink/blue/peach, D), 2 balls.

NEEDLES

U.S. size 8 (5 mm) and U.S. size 10 (6 mm). Adjust needle size if necessary to obtain the correct gauge.

NOTIONS

Tapestry needle; two 1" (2.5 cm) mother-of-pearl buttons.

GAUGE

16 sts and 24 rows = 4" (10 cm) in lace pattern with 2 strands of C held tog on larger needles.

NOTES

* Written instructions and a chart are both for the lace pattern; choose your favorite way of working lace.
* When changing color, it isn't necessary to weave in any yarn ends; these are knotted and trimmed to make the fringe. When joining a new yarn, leave a 4" (10 cm) tail for fringe.
* Grace and Impressions yarns are used double throughout.

Chart key:

- ☐ k on RS, p on WS
- • p on RS, k on WS
- ℓ k tbl
- ╱ k2tog on RS, p2tog on WS
- ╲ p2tog on RS, k2tog on WS
- ╲ k2tog tbl
- ⋏ sl 1, k2tog, psso
- ○ yo
- ⌒ BO 1 st
- ☐ pattern repeat

- ⧖ RT: k2tog but do not drop sts from left needle, k first st again, drop both sts from left needle

LACE SAMPLER

RIGHT BORDER

With 2 strands of A held tog and smaller needles, work picot CO as foll: *CO 5 sts using the cable method (see Glossary, page 117), BO 2 sts, slip st on right needle back to left needle—3 sts CO; rep from * until there are 48 sts on left needle.

Knit 1 row. Change to B and work 4 rows in garter st.

CENTER PANEL

Change to larger needles and 2 strands of C held tog and work 2 rows in garter st.

NEXT ROW: (WS) Change to 2 strands of D held tog and knit.

Work Rows 1–10 of lace chart 2 times, then cont garter st section or work Chart Rows 1–10 as foll:

CHART ROW 1: (RS) K3, yo, sl 1, k2tog, psso, yo, k5, yo, k2tog, k4, yo, k2tog, p1, k2, k2tog, yo, RT (see chart key), yo, k2tog through back loop (tbl), k2, p1, k3, [yo, p2tog] 2 times, yo, k1tbl, k2tog, p1, k2tog tbl, k1tbl, yo, k3.

CHART ROW 2: K3, p3, k1, p3, k2, [yo, p2tog] 2 times, k2, p10, k3, yo, k2tog, k4, yo, k2tog, k3, p3, k3.

CHART ROW 3: K3, yo, sl 1, k2tog, psso, yo, k5, yo, k2tog, k4, yo, k2tog, p1, k1, k2tog, yo, k4, yo, k2tog tbl, k1, p1, k3, [yo, p2tog] 2 times, yo, k1tbl, k2tog, p1, k2tog tbl, k1tbl, yo, k3.

CHART ROW 4: K3, p3, k1, p3, k2, [yo, p2tog] 2 times, k2, p10, k3, yo, k2tog, k4, yo, k2tog, k3, p3, k3.

CHART ROW 5: K3, yo, sl 1, k2tog, psso, yo, k5, yo,

k2tog, k4, yo, k2tog, p1, k2tog, yo, k1, k2tog, [yo] 2 times, k2tog tbl, k1, yo, k2tog tbl, p1, k3, [yo, p2tog] 2 times, yo, k1tbl, yo, k2tog, p1, k2tog tbl, yo, k4—49 sts.

CHART ROW 6: K4, p2, k1, p4, k2, [yo, p2tog] 2 times, k2, p4, k1, p5, k3, yo, k2tog, k4, yo, k2tog, k3, p3, k3.

CHART ROW 7: K3, yo, sl 1, k2tog, psso, yo, k5, yo, k2tog, k4, yo, k2tog, p1, k2, yo, k2tog tbl, k2, k2tog, yo, k2, p1, k3, [yo, p2tog] 2 times, yo, k1tbl, k1, k1tbl, yo, sl 1, k2tog, psso, yo, k5—50 sts.

CHART ROW 8: K5, p7, k2, [yo, p2tog] 2 times, k2, p10, k3, yo, k2tog, k4, yo, k2tog, k3, p3, k3.

CHART ROW 9: K3, yo, sl 1, k2tog, psso, yo, k5, yo, k2tog, k4, yo, k2tog, p1, k3, yo, k2tog tbl, k2tog, yo, k3, p1, k3, [yo, p2tog] 2 times, yo, k1tbl, k3, k1tbl, yo, k7—52 sts.

CHART ROW 10: BO 4 sts, k3 (3 sts on right needle), p7, k2, [yo, p2tog] 2 times, k2, p10, k3, yo, k2tog, k4, yo, k2tog, k3, p3, k3—48 sts rem.
Rep these 10 rows once more.

Garter stitch section

NEXT ROW: (RS) Knit.

With 2 strands of C held tog, work 2 rows in garter st.

With B, work 2 rows in garter st.

With 2 strands of A held tog, work 4 rows in garter st.

NEXT ROW: (WS) K3, *yo, p2tog; rep from * to last 3 sts, k3.

Work 3 rows in garter st.

With B, work 2 rows in garter st.

NEXT ROW: (WS) With 2 strands of C held tog, knit.

Work Rows 1–10 of lace chart once, or rep Chart Rows 1–10 above.

NEXT ROW: (RS) Knit.
With 2 strands of D held tog, work 4 rows in garter st.
With 2 strands of A held tog, work 2 rows in garter st.
With B, work 3 rows in garter st.

NEXT ROW: (RS) K3, *yo, k2tog; rep from * to last 3 sts, k3.

NEXT ROW: K3, purl to last 3 sts, k3.

NEXT ROW: (RS) K3, purl to last 3 sts, k3.

Rep from beg of center panel section until piece measures 38½ (43, 48)" (98 [109, 122] cm) from CO, ending with a RS row.

LEFT BORDER

With 2 strands of C held tog, work 2 rows in garter st.

Change to smaller needles.

With B, work 4 rows in garter st.

With 2 strands of A held tog, work 2 rows in garter st.

Work picot BO as foll: BO 3 sts, *slip st from right needle to left needle, CO 2 sts, BO 5 sts—3 sts dec; rep from * to end.

SHOULDER EDGING

Turn knitted piece ¼ turn counterclockwise, so that the right edge becomes the top.

With RS facing, smaller needles, and 2 strands of A held tog, pick up and knit 129 (139, 159) sts along top edge.

Work 4 rows in garter st, ending with a RS row.

NEXT ROW: (WS) K1, p1, *yo, p2tog; rep from * to last st, k1.

Work 2 rows in garter st.

NEXT ROW: (dec row) K3 (3, 2), *k2tog, k9; rep from * to last 5 (4, 3) sts, k2tog, k3 (2, 1)—117 (126, 144) sts rem.

NEXT ROW: Knit.

Work picot BO as foll: BO 3 sts, *slip st from right needle to left needle, CO 2 sts, BO 5 sts—3 sts dec; rep from * to end.

FINISHING

Knot fringe lengths and trim to desired length.

With RS facing, sew buttons onto left border, placing the first at the top corner and the second 4" (10 cm) down

textured + MODERN

ORGANIC · URBAN · SASSY · TWIST · METAL

The stitches and fabrics in this section reflect the modern woman—turning traditional knitting techniques on their sides, taking the classic cable in a new direction, and experimenting with unconventional constructions.

The yarns, ranging from crisp cotton to intricate bouclé and delicate mohair to glittering silver, push the edge of the traditional Aran texture and create a style as diverse as today's knitter.

piper PURSE

This bag began as a design experiment when I charted out and knitted an Aran pattern. I decided to turn the resulting piece of fabric on its side, sending the traditional cables in an entirely new direction. Transform your knitting experiment into an unexpected accessory by seaming two sides together, adding simple garter stitch, and finishing it with curved bag handles.

FINISHED SIZE

About 11½" (29 cm) wide and 11" (28 cm) tall, excluding handles.

YARN

Worsted weight (#4 Medium).

SHOWN HERE

Louisa Harding Nautical Cotton (100% mercerized cotton; 93 yd [85 m]/50 g): #4 gray, 4 balls.

NEEDLES

U.S. size 6 (4 mm), U.S. size 7 (4.5 mm), and U.S. size 8 (5 mm). Adjust needle size if necessary to obtain the correct gauge.

NOTIONS

Cable needle (cn); tapestry needle; 2 curved bag handles, 8½" (21.5 cm) wide and 5" (12.5 cm) tall.

GAUGE

27 sts and 28 rows = 4" (10 cm) in cable patt on largest needles.

Cable

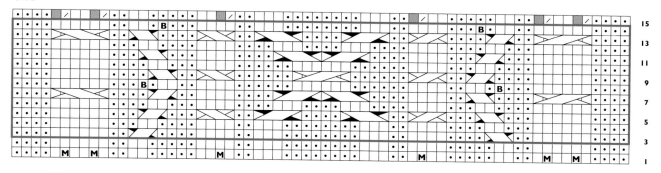

☐	k on RS, p on WS
·	p on RS, k on WS
╱	k2tog
M	M1 (see Glossary, page 122)
B	MB: see Stitch Guide
▨	no stitch
☐	pattern repeat

2/1 **RPC**: sl 1 st onto cn and hold in back, k2, p1 from cn

2/1 **LPC**: sl 2 sts onto cn and hold in front, p1, k2 from cn

2/2 **RC**: sl 2 sts onto cn and hold in back, k2, k2 from cn

2/2 **LC**: sl 2 sts onto cn and hold in front, k2, k2 from cn

3/2 **RPC**: sl 2 sts onto cn and hold in back, k3, p2 from cn

3/2 **LPC**: sl 3 sts onto cn and hold in front, p2, k3 from cn

3/3 **RC**: sl 3 sts onto cn and hold in back, k3, k3 from cn

3/3 **LC**: sl 3 sts onto cn and hold in front, k3, k3 from cn

alicia
TABARD

This simple sleeveless tunic is crossed with a bold braided cable that travels from hip to shoulder on front and back. I created this design to play with increasing and decreasing stitches, which make the cable panels for the front and back travel in opposite diagonal directions. Worked in luxurious yarn with a hint of shimmer, the unfussy shape creates a stylish silhouette.

FINISHED SIZE

33½ (38, 42½, 47)" (85 [96.5, 108, 119.5] cm) bust circumference. Tabard shown measures 33½" (85 cm).

YARN

DK weight (#3 Light).

SHOWN HERE

Louisa Harding Grace (50% merino wool, 50% silk; 110 yd [101 m]/50 g): #3 dove (gray), 9 (10, 11, 12) balls.

NEEDLES

U.S. sizes 6 (4 mm) and 7 (4.5 mm). Adjust needle size if necessary to obtain the correct gauge.

NOTIONS

Cable needle (cn); markers (m); removable markers; tapestry needle.

GAUGE

22 sts and 30 rows = 4" (10 cm) in patt st on larger needles. 32 sts and 32 rows of cable chart = 4" (10 cm) on larger needles.

NOTES

* On the back, the "move cable" row shifts the cable chart to the right by decreasing a stitch before the chart and increasing a stitch after the chart. On the front, the cable chart is shifted to the left by increasing a stitch before the chart and decreasing a stitch after the chart.
* The "move cable" row also creates a purl ridge in the stockinette stitch section of the fabric.

Cable

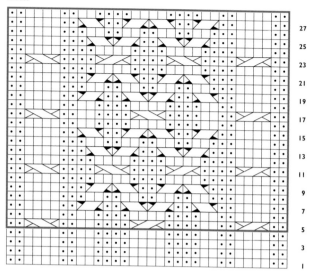

27
25
23
21
19
17
15
13
11
9
7
5
3
1

☐ k on RS, p on WS

• p on RS, k on WS

☐ pattern repeat

⟋⟍ **2/1 RPC:** sl 1 st onto cn and hold in back, k2, p1 from cn

⟍⟋ **2/1 LPC:** sl 2 sts onto cn and hold in front, p1, k2 from cn

⟋⟍ **2/2 RC:** sl 2 sts onto cn and hold in back, k2, k2 from cn

⟍⟋ **2/2 LC:** sl 2 sts onto cn and hold in front, k2, k2 from cn

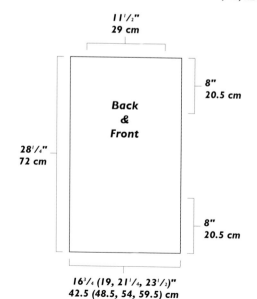

11¹⁄₂"
29 cm

8"
20.5 cm

Back & Front

28¹⁄₄"
72 cm

8"
20.5 cm

16³⁄₄ (19, 21¹⁄₄, 23¹⁄₂)"
42.5 (48.5, 54, 59.5) cm

BACK

With smaller needles, CO 92 (104, 116, 128) sts.

Work 9 rows in garter st.

NEXT ROW: (WS; inc row) K60 (66, 72, 78), [M1 (see Glossary, page 122), k1] 2 times, k2, M1, k5, M1, k1, M1, k5, M1, k3, M1, k1, M1, k13 (19, 25, 31)—100 (112, 124, 136) sts.

Change to larger needles.

ROW 1: (RS) K58 (64, 70, 76), place marker (pm), work next 32 sts according to cable chart, pm, k10 (16, 22, 28).

ROW 2: K6, purl to m, work according to chart to next m, purl to last 6 sts, k6.

ROW 3: Knit to m, work according to chart to next m, knit to end.

ROW 4: Repeat Row 2.

MOVE CABLE ROW: (RS) K6, purl to 2 sts before m, p2tog, work according to chart to next m, sl m, M1P (see Glossary, page 123), purl to last 6 sts, k6.

Cont as established, keeping first and last 6 sts in garter st, 32 sts between m in cable patt, and rem sts in St st (except on Move Cable Row; see Notes, page 51), rep move cable row every fourth row 47 more times—10 (16, 22, 28) sts before first m. Work 3 rows even.

Change to smaller needles.

NEXT ROW: (RS; dec row) K12 (18, 24, 30), [k2tog] 2 times, k2, k2tog, k4, [k2tog] 2 times, k4, k2tog, k2, [k2tog] 2 times, knit to end—92 (104, 116, 128) sts rem.

Work 8 rows in garter st.

With WS facing, BO all sts kwise.

FRONT

With smaller needles, CO 92 (104, 116, 128) sts.

Work 9 rows in garter st.

NEXT ROW: (WS; inc row) K60 (66, 72, 78), [M1, k1] 2 times, k2, M1, k5, M1, k1, M1, k5, M1, k3, M1, k1, M1, k13 (19, 25, 31)—100 (112, 124, 136) sts.

Change to larger needles.

ROW 1: (RS) K10 (16, 22, 28), pm, work next 32 sts according to cable chart, pm, k58 (64, 70, 76).

ROW 2: K6, purl to m, work according to chart to next m, purl to last 6 sts, k6.

ROW 3: Knit to m, work according to chart to next m, knit to end.

ROW 4: Repeat Row 2.

MOVE CABLE ROW: (RS) K6, purl to m, M1P, sl m, work according to chart to next m, p2tog, purl to last 6 sts, k6.

Cont as established, keeping first and last 6 sts in garter st, 32 sts between m in cable patt, and rem sts in St st (except on Move Cable Row; see Notes, page 51), rep move cable row every fourth row 47 more times—10 (16, 22, 28) sts after last m. Work 3 rows even.

Change to smaller needles.

NEXT ROW: (RS; dec row) K60 (66, 72, 78), [k2tog] 2 times, k2, k2tog, k4, [k2tog] 2 times, k4, k2tog, k2, [k2tog] 2 times, knit to end—92 (104, 116, 128) sts rem.

Work 8 rows in garter st.

With WS facing, BO all sts kwise.

FINISHING

With yarn threaded on a tapestry needle, use mattress stitch to sew shoulder seams, leaving 11½" (29 cm) open for neck. Place side slit markers along side edges of front and back 8" (20.5 cm) up from CO edge and place armhole markers along side edges of front and back 8" (20.5 cm) below shoulder seams. Sew side seams between markers.

emilie
HAT

This design is inspired by the cute little pixie hats popular in the 1940s and 1950s, though the glint of silver in the yarn is anything but old-fashioned. I took the idea of a knitted hood from my small collection of vintage knitting patterns as my starting point to update the pixie hat.

FINISHED MEASUREMENTS

12" (30.5 cm) circumference, relaxed. Hat will stretch to fit an average-size woman's head.

YARN

Worsted weight (#4 Medium).

SHOWN HERE

Louisa Harding Impression (16% kid mohair, 84% polyamid; 154 yd [141 m]/50 g): #11 thunder (gray), 1 ball.

NEEDLES

U.S. size 3 (3.25 mm): 16" (40 cm) circular (cir); U.S. size 6 (4 mm): 16" (40 cm) cir and set of 4 or 5 double-pointed (dpn). Adjust needle size if necessary to obtain the correct gauge.

NOTIONS

Marker (m); cable needle (cn); tapestry needle.

GAUGE

37 sts and 36 rnds = 4" (10 cm) in cable patt on larger needles.

NOTES

* Written instructions and a chart are both included for the cable pattern; choose your favorite way of working cables.
* The number of stitches in the cables decreases toward the top of the hat, which shapes the crown into a point.

Cable

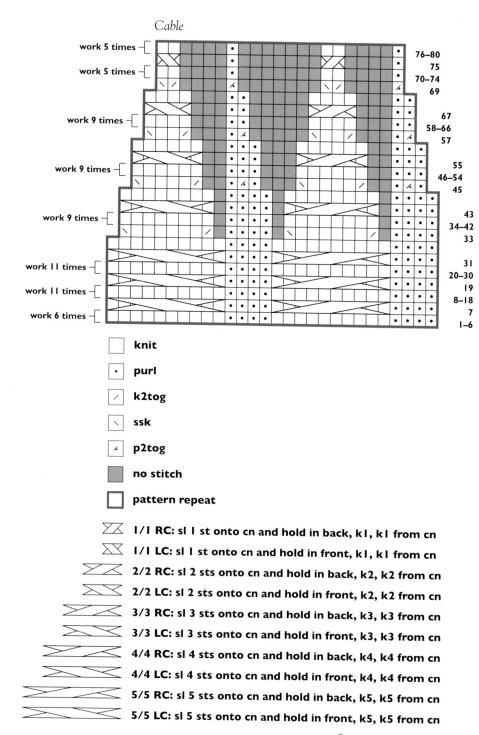

work 5 times · 76–80
· 75
work 5 times · 70–74
69

work 9 times · 67
58–66
57

work 9 times · 55
46–54
45

work 9 times · 43
34–42
33

work 11 times · 31
20–30
work 11 times · 19
8–18
work 6 times · 7
1–6

☐	knit
·	purl
╱	k2tog
╲	ssk
⋏	p2tog
▨	no stitch
☐	pattern repeat

1/1 RC: sl 1 st onto cn and hold in back, k1, k1 from cn

1/1 LC: sl 1 st onto cn and hold in front, k1, k1 from cn

2/2 RC: sl 2 sts onto cn and hold in back, k2, k2 from cn

2/2 LC: sl 2 sts onto cn and hold in front, k2, k2 from cn

3/3 RC: sl 3 sts onto cn and hold in back, k3, k3 from cn

3/3 LC: sl 3 sts onto cn and hold in front, k3, k3 from cn

4/4 RC: sl 4 sts onto cn and hold in back, k4, k4 from cn

4/4 LC: sl 4 sts onto cn and hold in front, k4, k4 from cn

5/5 RC: sl 5 sts onto cn and hold in back, k5, k5 from cn

5/5 LC: sl 5 sts onto cn and hold in front, k5, k5 from cn

HAT

BRIM

With smaller needle, CO 112 sts. Place marker (pm) and join for working in the rnd, being careful not to twist sts.

RND 1: [P4, k2, p2, k2, p2, k2] 8 times.

Rep Rnd 1 eleven more times.

CABLE SECTION

Change to larger needle and beg 12 rnd cable patt (or work Rows 1–80 of cable chart and proceed to Shape Point):

RND 1: [P4, k10] 8 times.

Rep Rnd 1 five more times.

RND 7: [P4, 5/5 RC, p4, 5/5 LC] 4 times.

RNDS 8–12: [P4, k10] 8 times.

Work Rnds 1–12 once more, then work Rnds 1–8 again.

NEXT RND: (dec rnd) [P4, k2tog, k6, ssk (see Glossary, page 119)] 8 times—96 sts rem.

NEXT RND: [P4, k8] 8 times.

Work even in patt for 8 more rnds.

NEXT RND: [P4, 4/4 RC, p4, 4/4 LC] 4 times.

NEXT RND: [P4, k8] 8 times.

NEXT RND: (dec rnd) [P1, p2tog, p1, k2tog, k4, ssk] 8 times—72 sts rem.

NEXT RND: [P3, k6] 8 times.

Work even in patt for 8 more rnds.

NEXT RND: [P3, 3/3 RC, p3, 3/3 LC] 4 times.

NEXT RND: [P3, k6] 8 times.

NEXT RND: (dec rnd) [P2tog, p1, k2tog, k2, ssk] 8 times—48 sts rem.

NEXT RND: [P2, k4] 8 times.

Work even in patt for 8 more rnds.

NEXT RND: [P2, 2/2 RC, p2, 2/2 LC] 4 times.

NEXT RND: [P2, k4] 8 times.

NEXT RND: (dec rnd) [P2tog, k2tog, ssk] 8 times—24 sts rem.

NEXT RND: [P1, k2] 8 times.

Work even in patt for 4 more rnds.

NEXT RND: [P1, 1/1 RC, p1, 1/1 LC] 4 times.

NEXT RND: [P1, k2] 8 times.
Work even in patt for 4 more rnds.

SHAPE POINT

NEXT RND: *K2tog; rep from * to end—12 sts rem.

NEXT RND: Knit.

NEXT RND: *K2tog; rep from * to end—6 sts rem.

NEXT RND: Knit.

NEXT RND: *K2tog; rep from * to end—3 sts rem.

I-CORD

Work 3-st I-cord (see Glossary, page 123) for 5" (12.5 cm).

BO all sts.

FINISHING

With rem yarn, make a 3" (7.5 cm) tassel (see Glossary, page 121) and attach to end of I-cord. Weave in loose ends.

belle
SCARF & WRAP

This design uses yarns from opposite ends of the spectrum to create distinctly fresh effects: The long scarf is knitted in a metallic silver ribbon to create a slinky, steely piece, while the wrap on page 63 is worked in a soft, fuzzy yarn. The stitch pattern has cables on the sides, which creates an uneven edge and gives the pieces a modern, almost futuristic feel.

FINISHED SIZE

scarf (opposite): About 5¾" (14.5 cm) wide and 71" (180.5 cm) long.
wrap (page 63): About 9½" (24 cm) wide and 35½" (90 cm) long.

YARN

scarf: Worsted weight (#4 Medium).
wrap: Chunky weight (#5 Bulky).

SHOWN HERE

scarf: Louisa Harding Glisten (97% nylon, 3% polyester; 93 yd [85 m]/50 g): #2 silver, 6 balls.
wrap: Louisa Harding Thalia (52% polyamid, 24% acrylic, 12% mohair, 6% wool, 6% metallic; 93 yd [85 m]/50 g): #1 natural, 3 hanks.

NEEDLES

scarf: U.S. size 8 (5 mm).
wrap: U.S. size 11 (8 mm).
Adjust needle size if necessary to obtain the correct gauge.

NOTIONS

Cable needle (cn); fine-eyed tapestry needle; eight ¾" (2 cm) mother-of-pearl buttons (wrap only).

GAUGE

scarf: 28 sts and 30 rows = 4" (10 cm) in cable patt.
wrap: 17 sts and 18 rows = 4" (10 cm) in cable patt.

Cable

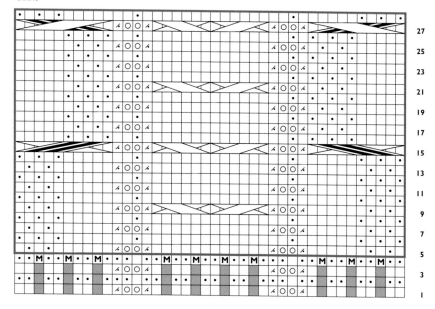

27								
25								
23								
21								
19								
17								
15								
13								
11								
9								
7								
5								
3								
1								

☐	k on **RS**, p on **WS**
·	p on **RS**, k on **WS**
⟋	p2tog
○	yo
M	M1 (see Glossary, page 121)
▨	no stitch
☐	pattern repeat

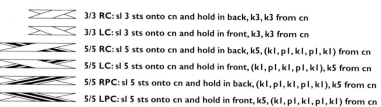

3/3 **RC**: sl 3 sts onto cn and hold in back, k3, k3 from cn

3/3 **LC**: sl 3 sts onto cn and hold in front, k3, k3 from cn

5/5 **RC**: sl 5 sts onto cn and hold in back, k5, (k1, p1, k1, p1, k1) from cn

5/5 **LC**: sl 5 sts onto cn and hold in front, (k1, p1, k1, p1, k1), k5 from cn

5/5 **RPC**: sl 5 sts onto cn and hold in back, (k1, p1, k1, p1, k1), k5 from cn

5/5 **LPC**: sl 5 sts onto cn and hold in front, k5, (k1, p1, k1, p1, k1) from cn

SCARF

CO 30 sts. Knit 1 row.

Work Rows 1–4 of cable chart—40 sts.

Rep Rows 5–28 of chart until piece measures 70" (178 cm) from CO, ending with a RS row.

NEXT ROW: (WS; dec row) K2, [k2tog, k1] 3 times, k1, p1, k2tog, k1, k2tog, k2, k2tog, k1, k2tog, k3, p1, [k1, k2tog] 3 times, k2—30 sts rem.

NEXT ROW: (RS) K7, p2tog, yo twice, p2tog, k8, p2tog, yo twice, p2tog, k7.

NEXT ROW: K9, p1, k11, p1, k8.

Work last 2 rows once more.

NEXT ROW: (RS) Knit.

BO all sts kwise.

WRAP

Work as for scarf until piece measures 34" (86.5 cm) from CO, ending with a RS row. Beg with dec row, work next 4 rows as for scarf. Work last 2 rows as foll:

NEXT ROW: (WS; buttonhole row) K1, yo, k2tog, k3, yo, p3tog, yo twice, p2tog, k2tog, yo, k4, yo, k2tog, p2tog, yo twice, p3tog, yo, k3, k2tog, yo, k1.

NEXT ROW: (RS) Knit.

BO all sts kwise.

FINISHING

Weave in loose ends. For wrap, sew buttons onto the CO edge to correspond with buttonholes on BO edge.

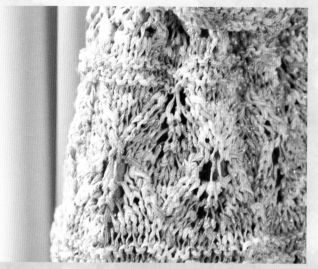

pretty + FEMININE

LUXURY · SOFT · INTRICATE · DELICATE · GRACEFUL

Blend undeniably feminine colors with luxurious touch and texture and be inspired by all things "girly"—clothes and accessories that make us feel special from the inside out.

Like a scene from an old-time movie, a spray of glamorous scent, or the opening of an expensive box of chocolates, the designs in this chapter evoke and embrace the glamorous side of women, the little things that make us feel pretty and feminine.

catherine
PURSE

This lacy purse is such a versatile pattern—it can be knitted using a wide variety of yarns, in stripes or in a single color, to make something elegant for evening or flirty and colorful to carry every day. For an evening purse, use a fingering-weight yarn to emphasize the delicate lace pattern. A coordinating silk lining gives the purse extra stability and a colorful treat on the inside.

FINISHED SIZE

About 16½" (42 cm) in circumference and 11" (28 cm) tall.

YARN

Worsted weight (#4 Medium).

SHOWN HERE

striped purse (opposite): Louisa Harding Glisten (97% nylon, 3% polyester; 93 yd [85 m]/50 g): #2 silver and #1 white, 1 ball each; and Louisa Harding Kashmir Aran (55% merino wool, 10% cashmere, 35% microfiber; 83 yd [76 m]/50 g): #1 cream, 1 ball.

glitter purse (page 70): Louisa Harding Glisten (97% nylon, 3% polyester; 93 yd [85 m]/50 g): #22 meadow (pink/green multi), 3 balls.

pink cotton purse (page 72): Louisa Harding Nautical Cotton (100% mercerized cotton; 93 yd [85 m]/50 g): #21 mauve, 3 balls.

NEEDLES

U.S. size 7 (4.5 mm). Adjust needle size if necessary to obtain the correct gauge.

NOTIONS

Tapestry needle; 7" (18 cm) square iron-on interfacing; 28" x 10" (71 cm x 25.5 cm) piece of lining fabric; sewing needle and thread; pins; iron.

GAUGE

22 sts and 28 rows = 4" (10 cm) in third lace patt with cream.

NOTE

* Written instructions and a chart are both included for the lace pattern; choose your favorite way of working lace.

STRIPED BAG

TOP SECTION

With silver, CO 127 sts.

Change to white and work 4 rows as foll:

ROW 1: (RS; dec row) K1, [k5, sl 1, k2tog, psso, k6] 9 times—109 sts rem.

ROW 2: Knit.

ROW 3: (dec row) K1, [k4, sl 1, k2tog, psso, k5] 9 times—91 sts rem.

ROW 4: Knit.

Work Rows 1–115 of drawstring purse chart, then proceed to finishing section or work rem sections as foll.

FIRST LACE SECTION

Change to cream.

ROW 1: K1, *[yo, k2tog through back loop (tbl)] 2 times, k1, [k2tog, yo] 2 times, k1; rep from * 8 more times.

ROW 2 AND EVERY WS ROW: Purl.

ROW 3: K1, [k1, yo, k2tog tbl, yo, sl 1, k2tog, psso, yo, k2tog, yo, k2] 9 times.

ROW 5: Rep Row 1.

ROW 7: Rep Row 3.

ROW 9: K1, [k2, yo, k2tog tbl, k1, k2tog, yo, k3] 9 times.

ROW 11: K1, [k3, yo, sl 1, k2tog, psso, yo, k4] 9 times.

ROW 12: Purl.

EYELET SECTION

Change to silver.

ROWS 1–3: Knit.

ROW 4: (WS) P1, *yo, p2tog; rep from * to end.

ROWS 5 AND 6: Knit.

Change to cream and, beg with a knit row, work 2 rows in St st.

With white, work 2 rows in garter st.

Drawstring Purse

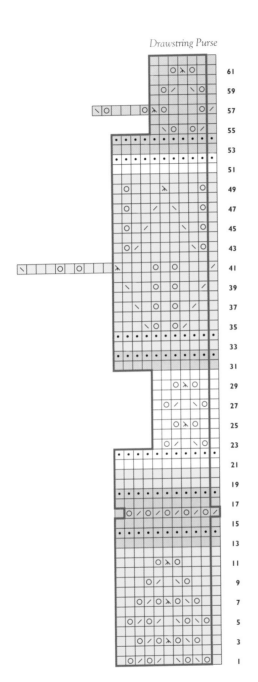

Drawstring Purse

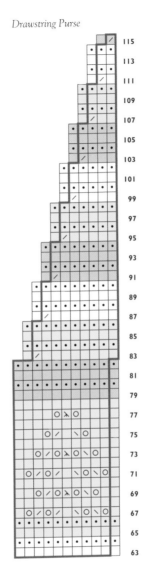

with cream, k on RS, p on WS

with cream, p on RS, k on WS

with cream, k2tog

with cream, k2tog tbl

with cream, sl 1, k2tog, psso

with cream, yo

with silver, k on RS, p on WS

with silver, p on RS, k on WS

with silver, k2tog on RS, p2tog on WS

with silver, k2tog tbl

with silver, sl 1, k2tog, psso

with silver, yo

with white, k on RS, p on WS

with white, p on RS, k on WS

with white, k2tog

with white, k2tog tbl

with white, sl 1, k2tog, psso

with white, yo

pattern repeat

SECOND LACE SECTION

ROW 1: K1, [yo, k2tog tbl, k1, k2tog, yo, k1] 15 times.

ROW 2 AND EVERY WS ROW: Purl.

ROW 3: K1, [k1, yo, sl 1, k2tog, psso, yo, k2] 15 times.

ROW 5: Rep Row 1.

ROW 7: Rep Row 3.

ROW 8: Purl.

With silver, knit 2 rows.

With cream, knit 2 rows.

THIRD LACE SECTION

ROW 1: K1, [k2, k2tog, yo, k1, yo, k2tog tbl, k3] 9 times.

ROW 2 AND EVERY WS ROW: Purl.

ROW 3: K1, [k1, k2tog, k1, yo, k1, yo, k1, k2tog tbl, k2] 9 times.

ROW 5: K1, [k2tog, k2, yo, k1, yo, k2, k2tog tbl, k1] 9 times.

ROW 7: K2tog, [k3, yo, k1, yo, k3, sl 1, k2tog, psso] 8 times, k3, yo, k1, yo, k3, k2tog tbl.

ROW 9: K1, [yo, k2tog tbl, k5, k2tog, yo, k1] 9 times.

ROW 11: K1, [yo, k1, k2tog tbl, k3, k2tog, k1, yo, k1] 9 times.

ROW 13: K1, [yo, k2, k2tog tbl, k1, k2tog, k2, yo, k1] 9 times.

ROW 15: K1, [yo, k3, sl 1, k2tog, psso, k3, yo, k1] 9 times.

ROW 16: Purl.

With white, knit 2 rows.

With silver, knit 2 rows.

FOURTH LACE SECTION

ROW 1: K1, [k2tog, yo, k1, yo, k2tog tbl, k1] 15 times.

ROW 2 AND EVERY WS ROW: Purl.

ROW 3: K2tog, [yo, k3, yo, sl 1, k2tog, psso] 14 times, yo, k3, yo, k2tog tbl.

ROW 5: K1, [yo, k2tog tbl, k1, k2tog, yo, k1] 15 times.

ROW 7: K1, [k1, yo, sl 1, k2tog, psso, yo, k2] 15 times.

ROW 8: Purl.

With white, knit 2 rows.

With cream, knit 2 rows.

FIFTH LACE SECTION

With cream, work Rows 1–12 of first lace section.

With silver, knit 4 rows.

BASE

ROW 1: (RS; dec row) With cream, [k8, k2tog] 9 times, k1—82 sts rem.

ROWS 2–4: Knit.

ROW 5: (RS; dec row) With white, [k7, k2tog] 9 times, k1—73 sts rem.

ROWS 6–8: Knit.

ROW 9: (RS; dec row) With silver, [k6, k2tog] 9 times, k1—64 sts rem.

ROWS 10–12: Knit.

ROW 13: With cream, [k5, k2tog] 9 times, k1—55 sts rem.

ROWS 14–16: Knit.

ROW 17: With white, [k4, k2tog] 9 times, k1—46 sts rem.

ROWS 18–20: Knit.

ROW 21: With silver, [k3, k2tog] 9 times, k1—37 sts rem.

ROWS 22–24: Knit.

ROW 25: (RS; dec row) With cream, [k2, k2tog] 9 times, k1—28 sts rem.

ROWS 26–28: Knit.

ROW 29: (RS; dec row) With white, [k1, k2tog] 9 times, k1—19 sts rem.

ROWS 30–32: Knit.

ROW 33: (RS; dec row) With silver, [k2tog] 9 times, k1—10 sts rem.

FINISHING

Break yarn. Thread tail through rem sts, pull tight to gather, and fasten off inside.

With yarn threaded on a tapestry needle, sew side and base seam using mattress stitch, or backstitch if preferred (see Glossary, page 124).

PURSE LINING

Cut a circle 6¾" (17 cm) in diameter from the lining fabric for the base. Iron interfacing to WS of fabric to stiffen, trimming interfacing if necessary.

Cut a length of fabric 21" (53.5 cm) long and 10" (25.5 cm) wide. Fold it in half with RS tog. With thread and sewing needle, backstitch side edge, leaving a ½" (1.3 cm) seam allowance. With RS tog, sew circular base to lining.

With WS of lining held against WS of purse, slip lining inside purse. Turn under ½" (1.3 cm) seam allowance at top of lining, pinning into place just below eyelet row. Whipstitch lining to purse.

With white, make 2 twisted cords, each about 24" (61 cm) long (see Glossary, page 121).

Beg at opposite sides of purse, thread cords in and out of eyelet holes around top of purse. Knot ends, leaving long lengths as tassels.

PINK COTTON OR GLITTER PURSE

Work as for striped bag, using a single color throughout.

victoria
FINGERLESS MITTENS

These cozy fingerless mittens are so simple to knit, but the luxurious yarns and dainty lace edging make them a simply luxurious accessory. The gold and pink hues of the striped pair remind me of something worn by a princess in a fairy story, while the pink pair is classically feminine . . . so if you know anyone wanting to embrace her inner princess, these mittens would make the ideal gift.

FINISHED SIZE

6¼" (16 cm) circumference measured above thumb. Mittens will stretch to fit a woman's hand.

YARN

DK weight (#3 Light) and worsted weight (#4 Medium).

SHOWN HERE

striped mittens (opposite): Louisa Harding Grace (50% merino wool, 50% silk; 110 yd [101 m]/50 g): #2 soft gold (tan, A), 1 ball; Louisa Harding Glisten (97% nylon, 3% polyester; 93 yd [85 m]/50 g): #4 gold (B), 1 ball; and Louisa Harding Impression (16% kid mohair, 84% polyamid; 154 yd [141 m]/50 g): #13 faded (pink/beige/silver, C), 1 ball.

plain mittens (page 76): Louisa Harding Grace (50% merino wool, 50% silk; 110 yd [101 m]/50 g): #4 rose, 1 ball.

NEEDLES

U.S. sizes 3 (3.25 mm), 5 (3.75 mm), and 6 (4 mm). Adjust needle size if necessary to obtain the correct gauge.

NOTIONS

Markers (m); tapestry needle.

GAUGE

24 sts and 32 rows = 4" (10 cm) in St st on largest needles.

STITCH GUIDE

PICOT BO:

BO 3 sts, *slip st on right needle back to left needle, CO 2 sts, BO 5 sts; rep from * to end—3 sts BO each rep.

STRIPE SEQUENCE:

1 row B, 2 rows A, 1 row B, 4 rows C.

Rep these 8 rows for patt.

STRIPED MITTENS

RIGHT HAND

Eyelet edging

With A and middle-size needles, work picot CO as foll: *CO 5 sts using the cable method (see Glossary, page 117), BO 2 sts, slip st on right needle back to left needle—3 sts CO; rep from * to CO 39 sts total.

ROWS 1–5: With B, knit.

ROW 6: (WS) P1, *yo, p2tog; rep from * to end.

ROWS 7–9: Knit.

ROW 10: (WS; dec row) Knit to last 2 sts, k2tog—38 sts rem.

Change to C and, beg with a knit row, work 2 rows in St st.

Ribbed cuff

Change to smallest needles.

ROW 1: (RS) *K2 through back loop (tbl), p2; rep from * to last 2 sts, k2 tbl.

ROW 2: *P2 tbl, k2; rep from * to last 2 sts, p2 tbl.

Rep Rows 1 and 2 ten more times—piece measures about 4" (10 cm) from CO.

Striped section

Change to largest needles and beg stripe sequence (see Stitch Guide). Work 4 rows in St st.

Thumb gusset

Cont in stripe sequence, shape gusset as foll:

ROW 1: (RS) K20, place marker (pm), M1 (see Glossary, page 122), k3, M1, pm, k15—40 sts.

Beg with a purl row, work 3 rows in St st.

INC ROW: K20, sl m, M1, knit to m, M1, sl m, k15—2 sts inc'd.

Rep inc row every 4th row 3 more times—48 sts.

Beg with a purl row, work 3 rows in St st.

Divide for thumb

NEXT ROW: K33, turn.

NEXT ROW: P13.

Working on these 13 sts only and beg with a knit row, work 10 rows in striped St st as foll: 2 rows A, 2 rows C, 2 rows B, 2 rows A, 2 rows C.

With B, BO all sts using picot BO (see Stitch Guide).

With A threaded on a tapestry needle, sew edges of thumb tog.

Hand

With RS facing and B, beg at base of thumb, pick up and knit (see Glossary, page 123) 2 sts from base of thumb, then knit to end of row—37 sts.

NEXT ROW: Purl.

Beg with a knit row, work 10 rows in striped St st as foll: 2 rows A, 2 rows C, 2 rows B, 2 rows A, 2 rows C.

With B and middle-size needles, work 5 rows in garter st.

NEXT ROW: (WS; dec row) P1, *yo, p2tog; rep from * to end.

Work 4 rows in garter st.

With A, BO all sts using picot BO.

LEFT HAND

Work as for right hand to thumb gusset.

Thumb gusset

ROW 1: (RS) K15, pm, M1, k3, M1, pm, k20—40 sts.

Beg with a purl row, work 3 rows in St st.

INC ROW: K15, sl m, M1, knit to m, M1, sl m, k20—2 sts inc'd.

Rep inc row every 4th row 3 more times—48 sts.

Beg with a purl row, work 3 rows in St st.

Divide for thumb

NEXT ROW: (RS) K28, turn.

NEXT ROW: P13.

Cont as for right-hand thumb, then work hand as for right-hand.

FINISHING

With A threaded on a tapestry needle, sew side seams using mattress stitch or backstitch (see Glossary, page 124).

PLAIN MITTENS

Work as for striped mittens, working in one color throughout.

juliet SCARF

This light and airy scarf is knitted in a soft, luxurious angora blend. A rosette brooch knitted in the same sumptuous yarn and finished with a dainty mother-of-pearl button adds a feminine touch while holding the scarf in place. The perfect length to tuck inside a collar, this floaty lace piece is warm and delicate at the same time.

FINISHED SIZE
About 6½" (16.5 cm) wide and 37" (94 cm) long.

YARN
DK weight (#3 Light).

SHOWN HERE
Louisa Harding Kimono Angora Pure (70% angora, 25% wool, 5% nylon; 125 yd [114 m]/25 g): #1 rice (tan), 1 ball.

NEEDLES
U.S. size 8 (5 mm). Adjust needle size if necessary to obtain the correct gauge.

NOTIONS
Tapestry needle; one ½" (1.3 cm) mother-of-pearl button; brooch back (available from craft or jewelry-supply store).

GAUGE
20 sts and 26 rows = 4" (10 cm) in lace patt.

NOTES
* The scarf shown here uses only one ball of yarn; knit the rosette first to ensure that you have enough yarn to complete it. Then work the scarf until the remaining yarn is used up.
* The needles used for this pattern are larger than indicated on the ball band. To change the scale of the lace pattern, use a different weight of yarn, but use a larger needle than usual for the yarn.

Lace

	k on RS, p on WS
·	p on RS, k on WS
╱	k2tog on RS
↗	k2tog on WS
╲	ssk
⋏	sl 1, k2tog, psso
o	yo
	pattern repeat

ROSETTE

CO 112 sts.

ROW 1: Knit.

ROW 2: K2, *k1, slip this st back onto left needle, lift the next 8 sts over this st and drop from needle, knit the first st again, k2; rep from * 9 more times—32 sts rem.

Work short-rows (see Glossary, page 125) as foll:

SHORT-ROW 1: K24, wrap and turn, k24.

SHORT-ROW 2: K16, wrap and turn, k16.

SHORT-ROW 3: K8, wrap and turn, k8.

Break yarn. Thread tail through rem sts, pull tightly to create a rosette, and secure with a few over-cast stitches.

SCARF

CO 31 sts. Knit 1 row. Work Rows 1–12 of lace chart, or work Chart Rows 1–12 below, until piece measures 37" (94 cm) from CO, or desired length, ending with a WS row, then proceed to final row.

CHART ROW 1: (RS) K6, yo, k2tog, k1, yo, k2, sl 1, k2tog, psso, k2, yo, k3, yo, k2tog, k3, [k2tog, yo] 2 times, k1, yo, k2—32 sts.

CHART ROW 2: K2, p9, k2, yo, k2tog, p9, k2, yo, k2tog, k4.

CHART ROW 3: K6, yo, k2tog, k2, yo, k1, sl 1, k2tog, psso, k1, yo, k4, yo, k2tog, k2, [k2tog, yo] 2 times, k3, yo, k2—33 sts.

CHART ROW 4: K2, p10, k2, yo, k2tog, p9, k2, yo, k2tog, k4.

CHART ROW 5: K6, yo, k2tog, k3, yo, sl 1, k2tog, psso, yo, k5, yo, k2tog, k1, [k2tog, yo] 2 times, k5, yo, k2—34 sts.

CHART ROW 6: K2, p11, k2, yo, k2tog, p9, k2, yo, k2tog, k4.

CHART ROW 7: K6, yo, k2tog, k1, yo, k2, sl 1, k2tog, psso, k2, yo, k3, yo, k2tog, k3, [yo, ssk] 2 times, k1, k2tog, yo, k2tog, k1—33 sts rem.

CHART ROW 8: K2, p10, k2, yo, k2tog, p9, k2, yo, k2tog, k4.

CHART ROW 9: K6, yo, k2tog, k2, yo, k1, sl 1, k2tog, psso, k1, yo, k4, yo, k2tog, k4, yo, ssk, yo, sl 1, k2tog, psso, yo, k2tog, k1—32 sts rem.

CHART ROW 10: K2, p9, k2, yo, k2tog, p9, k2, yo, k2tog, k4.

CHART ROW 11: K6, yo, k2tog, k3, yo, sl 1, k2tog, psso, yo, k5, yo, k2tog, k5, yo, sl 1, k2tog, psso, yo, k2tog, k1—31 sts rem.

CHART ROW 12: K2, p8, k2, yo, k2tog, p9, k2, yo, k2tog, k4.

Final row

Knit 1 row, then BO all sts kwise.

FINISHING

Sew button at the center of the rosette. Sew brooch back to back of rosette. Pin rosette to scarf.

charlotte
PURSE

This adorable evening purse is deceptively simple: The basic shape can be knitted in less than an hour, but the options for adding embellishment are endless. The finished bag can be customized in so many ways, with ribbons, rosettes, and vintage buttons from your stash. It's the perfect way to carry a little lipstick and your keys for an evening out.

FINISHED SIZE
About 5¾" (14.5 cm) wide and 9" (23 cm) long.

YARN
Chunky weight (#5 Bulky).

SHOWN HERE
Louisa Harding Thalia (52% polyamid, 24% acrylic, 12% mohair, 6% wool, 6% metallic; 93 yd [85 m]/50 g): #8 bisque (mauve/gray), 1 hank; a few yd (m) of yarn in complementary colors for flower decoration (at least 2 colors, MC and CC, for rosette and more colors as desired for small flowers).

NEEDLES
U.S. size 11 (8 mm). Adjust needle size if necessary to obtain the correct gauge.

NOTIONS
Tapestry needle; about seven ½–¾" (1.3–2 cm) mother-of-pearl buttons; 20" (51 cm) length of ⅝" (1.5 cm) wide velvet ribbon; sewing needle and thread.

GAUGE
14 sts and 19 rows = 4" (10 cm) in St st.

PURSE

CO 41 sts.

Work 2 rows in garter st.

Work 4 rows in St st.

Work 5 rows in garter st, ending with a RS row.

NEXT ROW: (WS) P2, *yo, p2tog; rep from * to last st, p1.

Work 4 rows in garter st.

Beg with a knit row, work in St st until piece measures 9" (23 cm) from CO, ending with a WS row.

BO all sts.

FINISHING

Fold piece in half with RS tog. With yarn threaded on a tapestry needle, sew bottom and side seam using backstitch (see Glossary, page 124).

Beg at opposite side of purse from side seam, thread ribbon through eyelets around top of purse.

Using sewing needle and thread, secure ends of ribbon to purse near eyelets with a few stitches. Sew buttons to ends of ribbon as shown at right. At side seam, pull out a loop of ribbon about 4" (10 cm) long for handle. Where loop of ribbon meets purse, sew a button through both layers of ribbon to keep handle from pulling through eyelets.

TWO-COLOR ROSETTE (MAKE 2)

With CC and needles to complement yarn, CO 112 sts. Change to MC.

ROW 1: Knit.

ROW 2: K2, *k1, slip this st back onto left needle, lift the next 8 sts over this st and drop from needle, knit the first st again, k2; rep from * 9 more times—32 sts rem.

Work short-rows (see Glossary, page 125) as foll:

SHORT-ROW 1: K24, wrap and turn, k24.

SHORT-ROW 2: K16, wrap and turn, k16.

SHORT-ROW 3: K8, wrap and turn, k8.

Break yarn. Thread tail through rem sts, pull tightly to create a rosette, and secure with a few overcast stitches.

SMALL FLOWERS

With CC and needles in size to complement scrap yarn, CO 36 sts.

ROW 1: *K1, BO 4 sts (2 sts on right needle); rep from * to end—12 sts rem.

Break yarn. Thread yarn through rem sts, pull tight to gather, and secure with a few overcast stitches.

ATTACH FLOWERS TO PURSE

With needle and thread, sew a button to the center of each flower. Arrange flowers on purse and sew into place as shown at right.

diane
CARDIGAN

This pretty cardigan is the epitome of femininity. The simple lace borders, knitted in beautifully soft golden hues, create a sumptuous sweater that is the essence of understated glamour. For an exceptionally luxurious cardigan, use a luxury fiber such as silk or cashmere.

FINISHED SIZE

34 (36½, 38½, 40½, 43, 45)" (86.5 [92.5, 98, 103, 109, 114.5] cm) bust circumference. Cardigan shown measures 36½" (92.5 cm).

YARN

DK weight (#3 Light) and worsted weight (#4 Medium).

SHOWN HERE

Louisa Harding Impression (16% kid mohair, 84% polyamid; 154 yd [141 m]/50 g): #12 vanilla (tan/silver, A), 4 (5, 5, 6, 6, 7) balls; and Louisa Harding Grace (50% merino wool, 50% silk; 110 yd [101 m]/50 g): #2 soft gold (tan, B), 2 (2, 2, 2, 3, 3) balls.

NEEDLES

U.S. sizes 3 (3.25 mm) and 6 (4 mm). Adjust needle size if necessary to obtain the correct gauge.

NOTIONS

Stitch holder; tapestry needle; ¾" (2 cm) mother-of-pearl button.

GAUGE

22 sts and 30 rows = 4" (10 cm) in St st with A on larger needles.

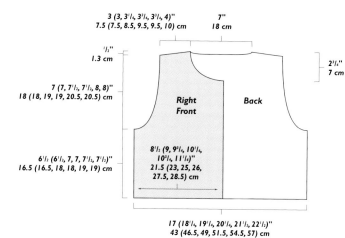

3 (3, 3¼, 3¾, 3¾, 4)"
7.5 (7.5, 8.5, 9.5, 9.5, 10) cm

7"
18 cm

½"
1.3 cm

2¾"
7 cm

7 (7, 7½, 7½, 8, 8)"
18 (18, 19, 19, 20.5, 20.5) cm

Right
Front

Back

6½ (6½, 7, 7, 7½, 7½)"
16.5 (16.5, 18, 18, 19, 19) cm

8½ (9, 9¾, 10¼,
10¾, 11¼)"
21.5 (23, 25, 26,
27.5, 28.5) cm

17 (18¼, 19¼, 20¼, 21½, 22½)"
43 (46.5, 49, 51.5, 54.5, 57) cm

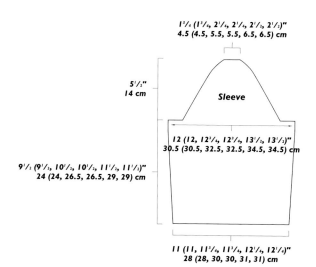

1¾ (1¾, 2¼, 2¼, 2½, 2½)"
4.5 (4.5, 5.5, 5.5, 6.5, 6.5) cm

5½"
14 cm

Sleeve

12 (12, 12¾, 12¾, 13½, 13½)"
30.5 (30.5, 32.5, 32.5, 34.5, 34.5) cm

9½ (9½, 10½, 10½, 11½, 11½)"
24 (24, 26.5, 26.5, 29, 29) cm

11 (11, 11¾, 11¾, 12¼, 12¼)"
28 (28, 30, 30, 31, 31) cm

BACK

With A and larger needles, CO 94 (100, 106, 112, 118, 124) sts.

Work eyelet edging as foll:

Work 3 rows in garter st.

NEXT ROW: (WS) P1, *yo, p2tog; rep from * to last st, p1.

Work 2 rows in garter st.

Beg with a knit row, work in St st until piece measures 6½ (6½, 7, 7, 7½, 7½)" (16.5 [16.5, 18, 18, 19, 19] cm) from CO, ending with a WS row.

SHAPE ARMHOLES

BO 4 (5, 7, 7, 8, 9) sts at beg of next 2 rows, then BO 3 (4, 4, 4, 5, 6) sts at beg of foll 2 rows—80 (82, 84, 90, 92, 94) sts rem.

DEC ROW: (RS) Ssk (see Glossary, page 119), knit to last 2 sts, k2tog—2 sts dec'd.

Rep dec row every other row 4 (4, 4, 5, 5, 5) more times—70 (72, 74, 78, 80, 82) sts rem.

Work even until armholes measure 7 (7, 7½, 7½, 8, 8)" (18 [18, 19, 19, 20, 20] cm), ending with a WS row.

SHAPE SHOULDERS AND BACK NECK

BO 5 (6, 6, 7, 7, 7) sts at beg of next 2 rows—60 (60, 62, 64, 66, 68) sts rem.

NEXT ROW: BO 5 (6, 6, 7, 7, 7) sts, knit until there are 9 (8, 9, 9, 10, 11) sts on right needle. Place 46 (46, 47, 48, 49, 50) sts from left needle onto a holder. Turn work.

NEXT ROW: BO 3 sts, work in patt to end—6 (5, 6, 6, 7, 8) sts rem.

BO all sts.

Replace held sts onto needle. With RS facing, rejoin A, BO 32 sts for neck, knit to end—14 (14, 15, 16, 17, 18) sts rem.

BO 5 (6, 6, 7, 7, 7) sts at beg of next row, then BO 3 sts at beg of foll row—6 (5, 6, 6, 7, 8) sts rem. BO all sts.

LEFT FRONT

With A and larger needles, CO 47 (50, 53, 56, 59, 62) sts.

Work eyelet edging as foll:

Work 3 rows in garter st.

NEXT ROW: (WS) P1, *yo, p2tog; rep from * to last 0 (1, 0, 1, 0, 1) st, p0 (1, 0, 1, 0, 1).

Work 2 rows in garter st.

Beg with a knit row, work in St st until piece measures 6½ (6½, 7, 7, 7½, 7½)" (16.5 [16.5, 18, 18, 19, 19] cm) from CO, ending with a WS row.

SHAPE ARMHOLE

BO 4 (5, 7, 7, 8, 9) sts at beg of next row, then BO 3 (4, 4, 4, 5, 6) sts at beg of foll RS row—40 (41, 42, 45, 46, 47) sts rem.

Work 1 row even.

Dec 1 st at armhole edge (beg of RS rows) on next row, then every other row 4 (4, 4, 5, 5, 5) more times—35 (36, 37, 39, 40, 41) sts rem.

Work even until armhole measures 5 (5, 5½, 5½, 6, 6)" (12.5 [12.5, 14, 14, 15, 15] cm), ending with a RS row.

SHAPE FRONT NECK

BO 10 sts at beg of next row, then BO 4 sts at beg of foll WS row—21 (22, 23, 25, 26, 27) sts rem.

Dec 1 st at neck edge (end of RS rows, beg of WS rows) every row 3 times, then every other row 2 times—16 (17, 18, 20, 21, 22) sts rem.

Work even until front measures same as back to shoulder, ending with a WS row.

SHAPE SHOULDER

BO 5 (6, 6, 7, 7, 7) sts at shoulder edge (beg of RS rows) 2 times—6 (5, 6, 6, 7, 8) sts rem.

Work 1 row even.

BO all sts.

RIGHT FRONT

Work as for left front to armhole shaping, ending with a RS row.

SHAPE ARMHOLE

BO 4 (5, 7, 7, 8, 9) sts at beg of next row, then BO 3 (4, 4, 4, 5, 6) sts at beg of foll WS row—40 (41, 42, 45, 46, 47) sts rem.

Dec 1 st at armhole edge (end of RS rows) on next row, then every other row 4 (4, 4, 5, 5, 5) more times—35 (36, 37, 39, 40, 41) sts rem.

Work even until armhole measures 5 (5, 5½, 5½, 6, 6)" (12.5 [12.5, 14, 14, 15, 15] cm), ending with a WS row.

SHAPE FRONT NECK

BO 10 sts at beg of next row, then BO 4 sts at beg of foll RS row—21 (22, 23, 25, 26, 27) sts rem.

Dec 1 st at neck edge (beg of RS rows, end of WS rows) every row 3 times, then every other row 2 times—16 (17, 18, 20, 21, 22) sts rem.

Work even until front measures same as back to shoulder, ending with a RS row.

SHAPE SHOULDER

BO 5 (6, 6, 7, 7, 7) sts at shoulder edge (beg of WS rows) 2 times—6 (5, 6, 6, 7, 8) sts rem.

Work 1 row even.

BO all sts.

SLEEVES

With A and larger needles, CO 60 (60, 64, 64, 68, 68) sts.

Work eyelet edging as for back.

Work 16 rows in St st, ending with a WS row.

Inc 1 st each end of needle on next row, then every 16th row 2 more times—66 (66, 70, 70, 74, 74) sts.

Work even until piece measures 9½ (9½, 10½, 10½, 11½, 11½)" (24 [24, 26.5, 26.5, 29, 29] cm) from CO, ending with a WS row.

SHAPE SLEEVE CAP

BO 5 (5, 6, 6, 7, 7) sts at beg of next 2 rows, then BO 3 sts at beg of foll 2 rows—50 (50, 52, 52, 54, 54) sts rem.

Dec 1 st each end of needle every row 3 times, then every other row 3 times—38 (38, 40, 40, 42, 42) sts rem.

Work 3 rows even.

Dec 1 st each end of needle on next row once, then every 4th row 4 times—28 (28, 30, 30, 32, 32) sts rem.

Work 1 row even.

Dec 1 st each end of needle on next row once, then every other row once, then next row once—22 (22, 24, 24, 26, 26) sts rem.

BO 3 sts at beg of next 4 rows—10 (10, 12, 12, 14, 14) sts rem.

BO all sts.

FINISHING

With A threaded on a tapestry needle, use backstitch (see Glossary, page 124) to sew shoulder seams. Sew in sleeves. Sew sleeve and side seams.

LACE EDGING

With B and larger needles, CO 12 sts.

FOUNDATION ROW: Knit.

ROW 1: (RS) K3, yo, k2tog, k1, k2tog, yo twice, k2tog, yo twice, k2—14 sts.

ROW 2: K3, p1, k2, p1, k4, yo, k2tog, k1.

ROW 3: K3, yo, k2tog, k1, k2tog, yo twice, k2tog, k4.

ROW 4: BO 2 sts, k3, (4 sts on right needle), p1, k4, yo, k2tog, k1—12 sts rem.

Rep Rows 1–4 until lace edging fits around bottom edge of cardigan from right front across back to left front. BO all sts.

With A, sew edging in place.

SLEEVE EDGING

Work lace edging until piece fits around bottom edge of sleeve beg at underarm seam.

With A, sew in place. Sew CO edge of lace to BO edge.

RIGHT FRONT BAND

With RS of right front facing, B, and smaller needles, pick up and knit 12 sts from lace edging and 65 (65, 71, 71, 75, 75) sts up to right front to neck—77 (77, 83, 83, 87, 87) sts total.

Edging

Work 2 rows in garter st.

NEXT ROW: (WS) P1, *yo, p2tog; rep from * to end.

Work 3 rows in garter st.

With WS facing, BO all sts kwise.

LEFT FRONT BAND

With RS of left front facing, B, and smaller needles, pick up and knit 65 (65, 71, 71, 75, 75) sts down left front to lace edging, pick up and knit 12 sts from lace edging—77 (77, 83, 83, 87, 87) sts total.

Work edging as for right front band.

NECK EYELET EDGING

With RS of right front facing, B, and smaller needles, pick up and knit 3 sts from right front band, 27 sts along right front neck to shoulder, 37 sts across back neck, 27 sts along left front neck, and 3 sts from left front band—97 sts total.

Work edging as for front bands.

CLOSURE

With A, sew button to top of left front eyelet edging. Use top eyelet in right front edging as buttonhole.

traditional + FOLK

WARMTH · COMFORT · TRADITION · BRIGHT · COLOR

Traditional stitch patterns like Fair Isle evoke old-fashioned values of
warmth and comfort, but these designs have a distinctly updated feminine
twist. Crisp colors and textures like silk and cotton show the patterns off
to their best advantage. Fair Isle may be traditional, but it doesn't need to
be stodgy! Play with yarn and make it modern.

jane SCARF

This scarf is knitted in a jewel-toned silk-merino blend, creating a colorful interplay of stripes, flowers, and diamonds. The color work is paired with subtle eyelets at the ends and raised ridges created by alternating knit and purl rows, which gives the piece dimension. This bright and cozy knit is perfect to warm you up on a dark winter day.

FINISHED SIZE

About 9¼" (23.5 cm) wide and 50¾" (129 cm) long.

YARN

DK weight (#3 Light).

SHOWN HERE

Louisa Harding Grace (50% merino wool, 50% silk; 110 yd [101 m]/50 g): #4 rose (pink, A), 2 balls; #7 petrol (teal, B), 1 ball; #13 aqua (C), 1 ball; #6 cherry (red, D), 2 balls; #9 espresso (brown, E), 1 ball; and #8 purple (F), 1 ball.

NEEDLES

U.S. size 5 (3.75 mm) and U.S. size 7 (4.5 mm). Adjust needle size if necessary to obtain the correct gauge.

NOTIONS

Tapestry needle.

GAUGE

22 sts and 33 rows = 4" (10 cm) in striped garter and St st patt on larger needles.

Fair Isle

37
35
33
31
29
27
25
23
21
19
17
15
13
11
9
7
5
3
1

+	with pink (A), k on RS, p on WS
×	with teal (B), k on RS, p on WS
I	with aqua (C), k on RS, p on WS
□	with red (D), k on RS, p on WS
•	with red (D), p on RS, k on WS
◣	with brown (E), k on RS, p on WS
○	with purple (F), k on RS, p on WS

SCARF

EDGING

With red and smaller needles, CO 51 sts.

ROWS 1–5: Knit.

ROW 6: (WS) P1, *yo, p2tog; rep from * to end.

ROWS 7–10: Knit.

FIRST FAIR ISLE SECTION

Change to larger needles. Work Rows 1–38 of Fair Isle chart.

STRIPED GARTER AND ST ST SECTION

ROW 1: (RS) With pink, knit.

ROW 2: With pink, k3, p45, k3.

ROWS 3–8: Rep Rows 1 and 2 three more times.

ROWS 9 AND 10: With teal, knit.

ROWS 11 AND 12: With aqua, knit.

ROWS 13 AND 14: With red, knit.

ROWS 15 AND 16: With aqua, knit.

ROWS 17 AND 18: With teal, knit.

ROWS 19–26: Rep Rows 1 and 2 four more times.

ROWS 27 AND 28: With brown, knit.

ROWS 29 AND 30: With purple, knit.

ROWS 31 AND 32: With red, knit.

ROWS 33 AND 34: With purple, knit.

ROWS 35 AND 36: With brown, knit.

Rep Rows 1–36 until piece measures 44" (112 cm) from CO, ending with a RS row.

NEXT ROW: (WS) With red, k3, p45, k3.

SECOND FAIR ISLE SECTION

Work Rows 1–38 of Fair Isle chart.

EDGING

Change to smaller needles.

ROWS 1–5: Knit.

ROW 6: P1, *yo, p2tog; rep from * to end.

ROWS 7–9: Knit.

With WS facing, BO all sts kwise.

FINISHING

Weave in loose ends.

mary BEANIE

This hat is an excellent introduction to Fair Isle knitting: The yarn is held double throughout, making it quick to knit up, and the two-color pattern creates a lovely result without juggling several strands of yarn. The finished hat is very warm and ideal for a knitted gift, especially for the holiday season.

FINISHED SIZE

About 20" (51 cm) circumference at lower edge and 19" (48.5 cm) circumference in Fair Isle area.

YARN

DK weight (#3 Light).

SHOWN HERE

Louisa Harding Grace (50% merino wool, 50% silk; 110 yd [101 m]/50 g): #4 rose (pink), 2 balls, and #6 cherry (red), 1 ball.

NEEDLES

U.S. size 9 (5.5 mm) and U.S. size 10 (6 mm). Adjust needle size if necessary to obtain the correct gauge.

NOTIONS

Size I/9 (5.5 mm) crochet hook; tapestry needle.

GAUGE

17 sts and 20 rows = 4" (10 cm) in Fair Isle patt on larger needles.

NOTE

Yarn is used double throughout.

HAT

BRIM

With 2 strands of pink held tog and smaller needles, CO 81 sts.

ROWS 1–4: Beg with a knit row, work in St st.

ROWS 5–6: Work in garter st.

ROWS 7–8: Work in St st.

FAIR ISLE SECTION

Change to larger needles. Work Rows 1–16 of Fair Isle chart.

Change to smaller needles. Cont in St st, work 2 rows pink, 1 row red, 1 row pink.

SHAPE CROWN

ROW 1: (RS, dec row) With pink, [k6, ssk (see Glossary, page 119)] 10 times, k1—71 sts rem.

ROWS 2 AND 4: With pink, purl.

ROW 3: With red, [k5, ssk] 10 times, k1—61 sts rem.

ROW 5: With pink, [k4, ssk] 10 times, k1—51 sts rem.

ROWS 6, 8, 10, AND 12: With red, purl.

ROW 7: With pink, [k3, ssk] 10 times, k1—41 sts rem.

ROW 9: With pink, [k2, ssk] 10 times, k1—31 sts rem.

ROW 11: With red, [k1, ssk] 10 times, k1—21 sts rem.

ROW 13: With red, [ssk] 10 times, k1—11 sts rem.

Break yarn, leaving a 12" (30.5 cm) tail. Thread tail through rem sts and pull tight to gather. With crochet hook and tail, make a chain (see Glossary, page 118, for crochet instructions) about 1½" (3.8 cm) long; sl st in first ch to form a loop. Fasten off.

FINISHING

Weave in loose ends. With yarn threaded on a tapestry needle, sew seam using mattress stitch or backstitch (see Glossary, page 124), reversing seam for lower ¾" (2 cm) for rolled brim.

Fair Isle

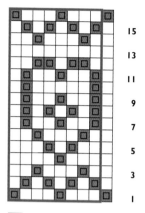

☐ with pink, k on RS, p on WS

▣ with red, k on RS, p on WS

☐ pattern repeat

emma
HAT

This design pairs a very traditional Fair Isle motif with a playful shape; its jester-like corners are finished with charming tassels. Worked in two different ways, the hat produces distinctly different results: The two-yarn version shows off the floral pattern dramatically and is perfect for a new Fair Isle knitter, while the five-yarn version delights with a subtler palette.

FINISHED SIZE

About 16½" (42 cm) circumference in Fair Isle area.

YARN

Worsted weight (#4 Medium).

SHOWN HERE

Five-color hat (opposite): Louisa Harding Kashmir Aran (55% merino wool, 10% cashmere, 35% microfiber; 83 yd [76 m]/50 g): #14 biscuit (tan), 2 balls; #8 olive, #6 lime, #15 lilac, and #2 sky (light blue), 1 ball each.

Two-color hat (page 107): Louisa Harding Kashmir Aran (55% merino wool, 10% cashmere, 35% microfiber; 83 yd [76 m]/50 g): #20 espresso (brown), 2 balls, and #2 sky (light blue), 1 ball.

NEEDLES

U.S. size 7 (4.5 mm), U.S. size 8 (5 mm), and U.S. size 9 (5.5 mm). Adjust needle size if necessary to obtain the correct gauge.

NOTIONS

Tapestry needle.

GAUGE

20 sts and 28 rows = 4" (10 cm) in St st on middle-size needles.

22 sts and 22 rows = 4" (10 cm) in Fair Isle patt on largest needles.

FIVE-COLOR HAT

RIBBED EDGING

With tan and smallest needles, CO 90 sts.

ROWS 1 AND 2: Work in garter st.

ROW 3: *K2, p2; rep from * to last 2 sts, k2.

ROW 4: *P2, k2; rep from * to last 2 sts, p2.

ROWS 5 AND 6: Rep Rows 3 and 4.

ROW 7: Rep Row 3.

ROW 8: *P2, k2; rep from * to last 2 sts, M1 (see Glossary, page 122), p2—91 sts.

FAIR ISLE SECTION AND BODY

Change to largest needles and work Rows 1–15 of five-color Fair Isle chart.

With tan and middle-size needles, beg with a purl row, work in St st until piece measures 9" (23 cm) from CO, ending with a WS row.

NEXT ROW: K44, k2tog (do not finish row). Fold hat in half with RS tog. Work three-needle BO (see Glossary, page 117) using largest needle for third needle.

TWO-COLOR HAT

With light blue and smallest needles, CO 90 sts. Change to brown and work as for five-color hat, working two-color Fair Isle chart in place of five-color Fair Isle chart, and using brown in place of tan after Fair Isle is complete.

FINISHING (BOTH HATS)

With tan or brown threaded on a tapestry needle, sew side seam using mattress stitch or backstitch (see Glossary, page 124). Using tan or brown, make two 4" (10 cm) tassels (see Glossary, page 121) and attach one at each top corner.

Five-color Fair Isle

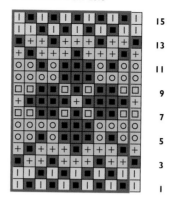

Two-color Fair Isle

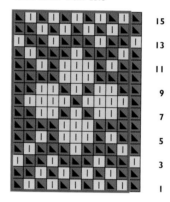

- ☐ tan
- ■ olive
- ⊞ lime
- ⊙ lilac
- ⊟ light blue
- ◥ brown
- ☐ pattern repeat

sarah
PURSE

The simple construction of this little purse lets the color and pattern take center stage. Worked in soft, chalky pastels, as shown here, it is at home on the beach. Worked in brighter shades, it's a fun and eye-catching tote for any season. You could even knit a different colorway on each side of the purse to make it reversible.

FINISHED SIZE

About 11¾" (30 cm) wide and 11½" (29 cm) tall, excluding handles.

YARN

Worsted weight (#4 Medium).

SHOWN HERE

Louisa Harding Nautical Cotton (100% mercerized cotton; 93 yd [85 m]/50 g): #2 natural (cream), 2 balls; #4 sky (blue), 1 ball; #13 flax (brown), 2 balls; #23 sage (green), 1 ball; and #3 rose (pink), 1 ball.

NEEDLES

U.S. size 5 (3.75 mm) and U.S. size 8 (5 mm). Adjust needle size if necessary to obtain the correct gauge.

NOTIONS

Tapestry needle; pair of 8" (20.5 cm) wide x 5½" (14 cm) high curved bag handles with slits.

GAUGE

20 sts and 24 rows = 4" (10 cm) in Fair Isle patt on larger needles.

BAG BODY

FIRST STRIPED FLAP

With cream and smaller needles, CO 59 sts. Working in garter st, work 2 rows in each of the foll colors: cream, blue, brown, green, pink.

FAIR ISLE SECTION

Change to larger needles and work Rows 1–34 of Fair Isle chart 2 times.

With cream, work 2 rows in garter st (to form fold line). Work Fair Isle chart in reverse 2 times, beg with Row 34 (worked as a RS row) and finishing with Row 1.

SECOND STRIPED FLAP

Change to smaller needles. Working in garter st, work 2 rows in each of the foll colors: pink, green, brown, blue. With cream, knit 1 row. With WS facing, BO all sts kwise.

FINISHING

Weave in loose ends. Fold purse in half at fold line. With yarn threaded on a tapestry needle and beg at fold line, sew side edges tog using mattress stitch or backstitch (see Glossary, page 124) to 4" (10 cm) from top, matching the Fair Isle patt on front and back.

Insert striped top section through slit in handle and sew down on inside of bag. Rep for other handle.

Fair Isle

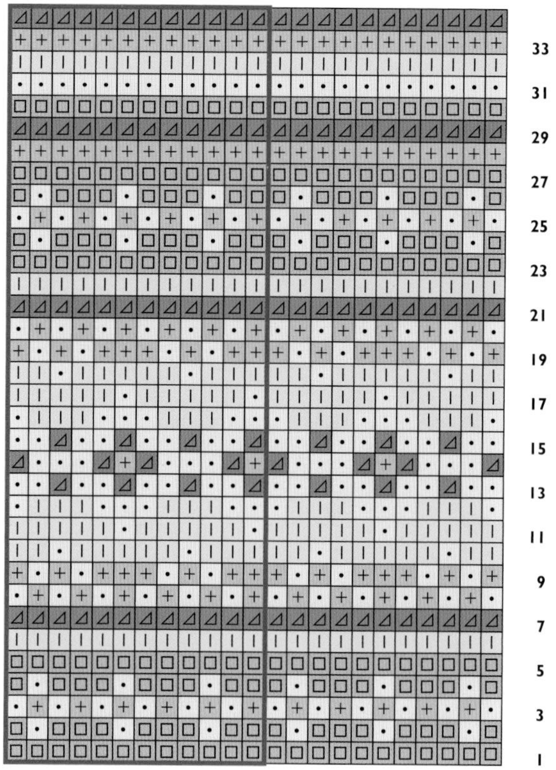

- · cream
- I blue
- □ brown
- ◿ green
- + pink
- ☐ pattern repeat

yarn information

You can purchase yarns two ways: from the yarn shop and from the Internet. There are many good Internet yarn sites, which you can find easily by searching for knitting yarns. These sites often show the whole spectrum of colors and types of yarn available, and they can be a fantastic resource. However, when you begin knitting, visit a yarn store first if possible to see what is available. There you will find helpful, knowledgeable staff as well as an amazing array of products like needles, buttons, beads, and most importantly, yarns. Nothing compares to the tactile quality of touching and feeling a ball of yarn—you will find such an amazing array of color and texture that you may feel like a kid in a candy shop.

With all these options, choosing which yarn to use can be quite daunting. Knowing about the properties of different kinds of fiber may help you decide.

ANIMAL FIBERS

Wool

Wool from the fleece of sheep is the traditional material for knitting yarn. It provides excellent insulation, making it very warm. Traditional wool can be scratchy, making it uncomfortable when worn close to the skin as a hat, scarf, or gloves. Many yarn producers now make very soft wool blends using different types of fleece. Wool can also be spun with synthetic yarn or treated to make it machine washable (or "superwash"). Check the label for washing instructions. To soften a piece knitted in traditional or slightly coarse wool, handwash it with some fabric softener.

Cashmere

Cashmere is a luxury fiber produced from the under-hair of Cashmere goats. Pure cashmere yarns can be expensive and pill heavily, so many producers combine it with wool or synthetics to make it more affordable. These yarns feel wonderful to knit with, touch, and wear.

Silk

Silk is an incredibly strong fiber created by silkworms, which produce a single long strand in each cocoon. It takes dye beautifully but is expensive to produce, so it is often blended with other fibers.

Mohair

Mohair comes from the Angora goat. It produces a light, fluffy, and very warm yarn with a "halo" of fine hairs. Because of this hairy property, it can be knitted to a surprisingly large gauge while still creating a stable fabric.

Angora

Angora comes from the Angora rabbit. The luxurious silky hairs are very short and difficult to spin without blending with wool or synthetic fibers. Though expensive to produce, it is ideal for small projects. (Be aware that some people can have an allergic reaction to angora.)

PLANT FIBERS

Cotton

Cotton yarns are soft, making them popular for sensitive skin and next-to-skin wear. The texture of bobbles or cables is often enhanced by the crispness of cotton, but it lacks elasticity and can be quite heavy. Cotton is ideal for small projects like purses, but it is important to maintain even tension for the project to wear well.

Linen

Linen is obtained from the flax plant. It is strong and extremely durable, but it can be tough and ropelike. Linen is often blended with other fibers to make it softer and easier to work with.

SYNTHETIC FIBERS

Nylon, acrylic, and rayon yarns are widely available
in the marketplace. These man-made fibers come in
many varieties, and you can find exciting "experimen-
tal" yarns in wonderful color combinations. I especially
love the metallic fibers that add sparkle and glamour to
many yarns. While they can be fun, these yarns will not
have the long-lasting properties of natural yarns.

SUBSTITUTING YARNS

In the patterns for this book I have used a variety of
different yarn types—some for practical reasons; some
because of the color, texture, or shine; and some because they are luxurious. You may wish to substitute a
yarn of your own choice, but please take care if you do
this. Each pattern has been created with the properties
of the specific yarn, including the gauge, in mind.

If you substitute a yarn, you must achieve the stated
gauge to create the correct size. Choose a yarn of about
the same weight (see chart below for more information
on yarn weights). It can be fun and inspiring to substitute yarns, but be sure to knit a swatch of your chosen
yarn before embarking on the pattern.

STANDARD YARN SIZES, NEEDLE SIZES, AND GAUGES

YARN WEIGHT	NEEDLE SIZE		GAUGE (STITCHES/4")
#1 Super Fine (fingering)	U.S. 1–3	2.25–3.25 mm	27–32
#2 Fine (sport)	U.S. 3–5	3.25–3.75 mm	23–26
#3 Light (DK)	U.S. 5–7	3.75–4.5 mm	21–24
#4 Medium (worsted)	U.S. 7–9	3.75 – 5.5 mm	16–20
#5 Bulky (chunky)	U.S. 9–11	5.5–8 mm	12–15

beg	beginning; begin; begins	*psso*	pass slipped stitch over
BO	bind off	*pwise*	purlwise, as if to purl
CC	contrasting color	*rem*	remain(s); remaining
cm	centimeter(s)	*rep*	repeat(s)
cn	cable needle	*rnd(s)*	round(s)
CO	cast on	*RS*	right side
cont	continue(s); continuing	*sl*	slip
dec(s)	decrease(s); decreasing	*sl st*	slip stitch (slip 1 stitch pwise unless otherwise indicated)
foll	following; follows		
g	gram(s)	*ssk*	slip 2 sts kwise, one at a time, from the left needle to right needle, insert left needle tip through both front loops and knit together from this position (1 st decrease)
inc(s)	increase(s); increasing		
k	knit		
k1f&b	knit into the front and back of same stitch		
k2tog	knit two stitches together	*St st*	stockinette stitch
k3tog	knit three stitches together	*st(s)*	stitch(es)
kwise	knitwise, as if to knit	*tbl*	through back loop
lb	pound	*tog*	together
m	marker(s)	*WS*	wrong side
MC	main color	*wyb*	with yarn in back
mm	millimeter(s)	*wyf*	with yarn in front
M1	make one (increase)	*yd*	yard(s)
oz	ounce(s)	*yo*	yarnover
p	purl	*	repeat starting point
p1f&b	purl into front and back of same stitch	**	repeat all instructions between asterisks
p2tog	purl two stitches together	( )	alternate measurements and/or instructions
patt(s)	pattern(s)	[ ]	instructions are worked as a group a specified number of times

BIND-OFFS

STANDARD BIND-OFF

Knit the first stitch, *knit the next stitch (two stitches on right needle), insert left needle tip into first stitch on right needle (Figure 1) and lift this stitch up and over the second stitch (Figure 2) and off the needle (Figure 3). Repeat from * for the desired number of stitches. If you find that the bound-off edge is too tight, try binding off with a larger needle than the one with which the piece was knitted.

FIGURE 1   FIGURE 2   FIGURE 3

THREE-NEEDLE BIND-OFF

Place stitches to be joined onto two separate needles. Hold the needles parallel. Insert a third needle into first stitch on each of the other two needles (Figure 1) and knit them together (Figure 2), *knit the next stitch on each needle together in the same way, then pass the first stitch over the second (Figure 3). Repeat from * until no stitches remain on the first two needles. Cut yarn and pull tail through the last stitch.

FIGURE 1   FIGURE 2   FIGURE 3

BLOCKING

PRESSING

Pressing the knitted fabric will help the pieces maintain their shape and give them a smooth finish. With the wrong side of the fabric facing, pin each knitted piece to the measurements given onto an ironing board. As each yarn is different, refer to the ball band and press pieces according to instructions.

CAST-ONS

CABLE CAST-ON

Make a slipknot and place it on the left needle for the first stitch. Insert the right needle into the stitch and knit it, but don't drop the old stitch from the left needle. Place the new stitch on the left needle. *Insert right needle between the first two stitches on left needle (Figure 1), wrap yarn around needle as if to knit, draw yarn through (Figure 2), and place new loop on left needle (Figure 3) to form a new stitch. Repeat from * for the desired number of stitches, always working between the first two stitches on the left needle.

FIGURE 1   FIGURE 2   FIGURE 3

LONG-TAIL CAST-ON

Leaving a long tail (about ½" [1.3 cm] for each stitch to be cast on),
make a slipknot and place on right needle. Place thumb and index
finger of your left hand between the yarn ends so that working yarn
is around your index finger and tail end is around your thumb.
Secure the yarn ends with your other fingers and hold your palm
upwards, making a V of yarn (Figure 1). *Bring needle up through
loop on thumb (Figure 2), catch first strand around index finger,
and go back down through loop on thumb (Figure 3). Drop loop
off thumb and, placing thumb back in V configuration, tighten
resulting stitch on needle (Figure 4). Repeat from * for the desired
number of stitches.

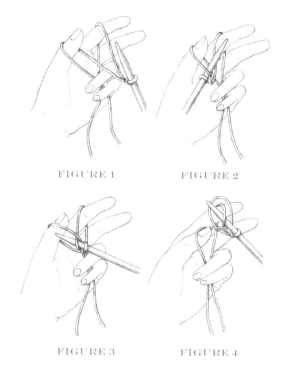

FIGURE 1   FIGURE 2

FIGURE 3   FIGURE 4

CHARTS

The instructions for several patterns in this book use both written
and visual instructions—charts. We use charts when writing out
the whole pattern would be very complicated. Once you begin to
visualize your knitting in relation to the chart, it becomes easier to
be creative with your knitting, as you can treat the knitted fabric as a
picture and "paint" with texture and color.

A chart represents each stitch as a box on a sheet of graph
paper; each square represents one stitch, and each line of squares
designates a row of knitting. The chart's symbols indicate how to
work each stitch.

Reading the chart is easier if you visualize it as the right side of
a piece of knitting, working from the lower edge to the top. When
knitting back and forth, read odd-numbered rows (which usually
indicate the right side) from right to left and even-numbered rows
(wrong side) from left to right. If you're knitting in the round,
read every row from right to left.

CROCHET CHAIN

Make a slipknot and place on crochet hook. *Yarn over hook and
draw it through loop on hook. Repeat from * for desired length.
To fasten off, cut yarn and draw tail through last loop formed.

DECREASES

K2TOG

Knit two stitches together as if they were a single stitch.

SSK

Slip two stitches individually knitwise (Figure 1), insert left needle tip into the front of these two slipped stitches, and use the right needle to knit them together through their back loops (Figure 2).

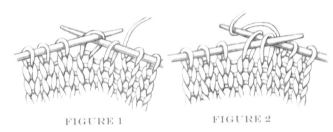

FIGURE 1   FIGURE 2

P2TOG

Purl two stitches together as if they were a single stitch.

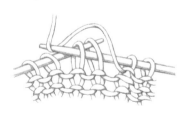

EMBELLISHMENTS

EMBROIDERY

Blanket stitch

Bring threaded needle out from back to front at the center of a knitted stitch. *Insert needle at center of next stitch to the right and two rows up, and out at the center of the stitch two rows below. Repeat from *.

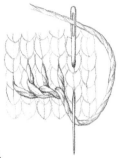

Duplicate stitch

Bring threaded needle out from back to front at the base of the V of the knitted stitch you want to cover. Working right to left, *pass needle in and out under the stitch in the row above it and back into the base of the same stitch. Bring needle back out at the base of the V in the next stitch to be covered. Repeat from * for the desired number of stitches.

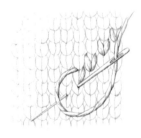

Lazy Daisy

With yarn threaded on a tapestry needle, bring the needle out from back to front at the center of a knitted stitch. *Form a short loop and insert needle back where it came out. Bring the needle from back to front inside the formed loop and pass it to the back outside the loop, securing the loop to the knitted fabric (Figure 1). Beginning each stitch at the same point on the knitted background, repeat from * several times to form a flower (Figure 2) or work singly to create a leaf. Lazy daisy stitch looks effective as self-colored embroidery or in contrast colors, using up remnants of yarn.

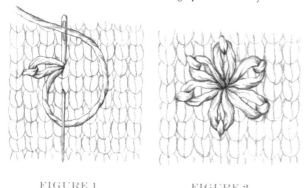

FIGURE 1   FIGURE 2

French Knots

With yarn threaded on a tapestry needle, bring the needle from the back to the front of the work and wind the yarn several times around the needle according to the size of knot required. Take the needle back near where it came out and draw the yarn through, forming a small knot on the right side of work.

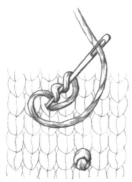

Running Stitch

Working small straight stitches, pass the threaded needle over one knitted stitch and under the next to form a dashed line. The stitches can be worked in equal or varying lengths, horizontally, vertically, or diagonally.

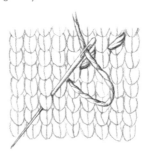

FRINGE

Cut strands of yarn to about 1" (2.5 cm) longer than twice the length of the desired finished fringe. Fold the yarn in half and use a crochet hook to pull just the folded part of the yarn through the knitted piece from back to front. Draw the yarn ends through the fold and pull snug. When you have placed all the desired fringe, trim the ends to even lengths.

POM-POMS

Cut two circles of cardboard, each slightly bigger than the size of the desired pom-pom. Cut a smaller hole in the center of each circle, about half the size of the original diameter—the larger this hole is, the fuller the pom-pom (Figure 1). Holding the two circles together, wind several strands of yarn through the ring until it is completely covered. (As the hole at the center fills up, you may find it easier to use a darning needle to pass the yarn through.) Cut between the two circles using a pair of sharp scissors, making sure all the yarn has been cut (Figure 2).

Separate the two circles slightly, wrap a strand of yarn between them, and knot firmly. Pull the two circles apart and fluff the pom-pom to cover the tie. Trim the pom-pom if necessary (Figure 3), but don't get carried away.

FIGURE 1

FIGURE 2

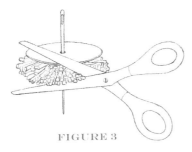

FIGURE 3

TWISTED CORD

Cut two lengths of yarn as specified in pattern. Knot the strands together at each end. Attach one end to a hook or door handle and insert a knitting needle through the other end. Twist the needle (Figure 1); the tighter the twist, the firmer the finished cord will be. Holding the cord in the center with one hand (you may need some help), bring both ends of cord together, allowing the two halves to twist together (Figure 2). Keep the cord straight and avoid tangling. Knot the cut ends together and trim.

FIGURE 1   FIGURE 2

TASSEL

Loop yarn around a stiff piece of cardboard that is the desired tassel length. Tie one end of the loops with a piece of yarn—this will be used to attach the tassel to the knitted piece (Figure 1). Slip the loops off the cardboard and tie another piece of yarn several times around the loops near the top. Secure the end of this yarn through the loops and down to the bottom of the tassel (Figure 2). Cut the lower ends to the desired length.

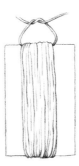

FIGURE 1   FIGURE 2

GARTER STITCH

Garter stitch produces a reversible textured fabric that is very elastic lengthwise. When working back in forth to produce flat pieces, knit every stitch of every row. When working circularly, alternate rows of all knit and all purl.

GAUGE

Gauge is an indispensable part of any knitting pattern. Each pattern is worked out mathematically, and if the correct gauge is not achieved the project will not fit as intended. Before embarking on knitting your garment, we recommend you check your gauge. Using the recommended needle size, cast on thirty to forty stitches and, in the pattern stitch specified in the instructions, work at least 4" (10 cm) from the cast-on edge. Remove the stitches from the needle or bind off loosely and lay the swatch on a flat surface. Place a ruler or tape measure across it and, in the space of 4" (10 cm), count the number of stitches across and rows down (including fractions of stitches and rows). Repeat this measurement in two or three places on the swatch to confirm your initial measurement. If you have more stitches and rows than called for in the pattern's instructions, try again using larger needles; if you have too few stitches or rows, try again with smaller needles. Note: Check your gauge regularly as you knit, as it can become tighter or looser as you become relaxed and confident with your knitting.

Some of the patterns include ribs, textured patterns, or cables, which can change the gauge substantially. The pattern will specify whether the gauge swatch should be worked in stockinette or another stitch.

I-CORD

Using 2 double-pointed needles, cast on the desired number of stitches (usually 3 to 4). *Without turning the needle, slide stitches to other end of needle, pull the yarn around the back, and knit the stitches as usual. Repeat from * for desired length.

INCREASES

KNIT ONE FRONT AND BACK (K1F&B)

Knit into a stitch but leave it on the left needle (Figure 1), then knit through the back loop of the same stitch (Figure 2) and slip the original stitch off the needle.

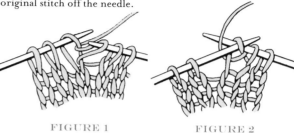

FIGURE 1   FIGURE 2

MAKE ONE (M1)

With left needle tip, lift the strand between last knitted stitch and first stitch on left needle from front to back (Figure 1), then knit the lifted strand through the back loop (Figure 2).

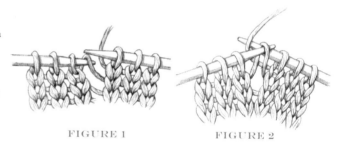

FIGURE 1   FIGURE 2

MAKE ONE PURLWISE (M1P)

With left needle tip, lift the strand between the last knitted stitch and the first stitch on the left needle from back to front (Figure 1). Purl the lifted loop (Figure 2).

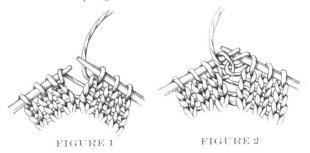

FIGURE 1   FIGURE 2

YARNOVER INCREASE (YO)

Wrap the working yarn around the needle from front to back (Figure 1), then bring yarn into position to work the next stitch (leave it in back if a knit stitch follows; bring it under the needle to the front if a purl stitch follows). To make a double yarnover increase ([yo] 2 times), wrap the yarn around the needle from front to back one time completely, then bring the yarn over the needle again before working the next stitch (Figure 2).

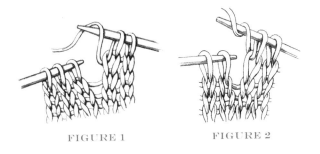

FIGURE 1   FIGURE 2

LACE KNITTING

The lace patterns in this book use yarnovers to create eyelets. Each yarnover usually corresponds to a decrease, so that the number of stitches remains constant at the end of each row. Some patterns are achieved by increasing stitches on some rows and decreasing them on subsequent rows. Although these patterns are quite complex, the effect is very rewarding.

PICK UP AND KNIT

Work from right to left with right side facing. For horizontal (bind-off or cast-on) edges: Insert tip of needle into the center of the stitch below the bind-off or cast-on edge (Figure 1), wrap yarn around needle, and pull it through to make a stitch on the needle (Figure 2). Pick up one stitch for every stitch along the horizontal edge. For shaped edges, insert needle between last and second-to-last stitches, wrap yarn around needle, and pull it through to make a stitch on the needle. Pick up about three stitches for every four rows along the shaped edge.

FIGURE 1   FIGURE 2

SEAMS

BACKSTITCH SEAM

With right sides together, pin the pieces to be joined together so that their edges are even. Insert the threaded needle from back to front through both pieces at the right-hand edge, take the yarn around the edges and reinsert the yarn through the same stitch, pulling tight to secure. *Insert the needle from back to front two stitches to the left (Figure 1), then from front to back one stitch to the right (Figure 2). Repeat from * to the end, pull the yarn firmly, and fasten off on the wrong side.

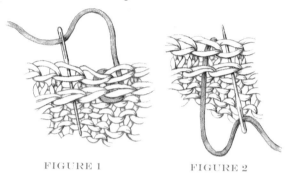

FIGURE 1   FIGURE 2

EDGE TO EDGE STITCH

With right sides facing up and the two pieces to be joined lying edge to edge, insert a threaded tapestry needle from front to back through one stitch at the edge of one piece, then bring the needle back up through the corresponding stitch on the other piece. *Insert the needle from front to back in the next stitch on the first piece and bring the needle from back to front in the corresponding stitch on the second piece. Working in a circular motion, repeat from * to the end, pulling the yarn in the direction of the seam. Pull the yarn firmly and fasten off inside.

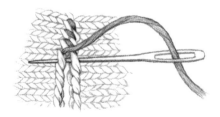

MATTRESS STITCH

This seam, worked on the right side of the fabric, is ideal for matching stripes. Mattress stitch should be worked one stitch in from the edge to give the best finish. With the right sides facing and the two pieces to be joined lying edge to edge, use a threaded tapestry needle to pick up one bar between the first two stitches on one piece (Figure 1). Take the needle to the front of the opposite piece and lift the corresponding bar plus the bar above it (Figure 2). *Pick up the next two bars on the first piece, then the next two bars on the other (Figure 3). Repeat from * to the end, pulling the yarn in the direction of the seam. Finish by picking up the last bar or pair of bars at the top of the first piece. Pull the yarn firmly and fasten off inside.

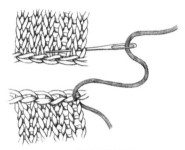

FIGURE 1

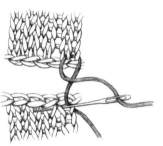

FIGURE 2

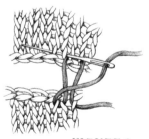

FIGURE 3

SHORT-ROWS

Work to turning point, slip next stitch purlwise to right needle, (Figure 1), then bring the yarn to the front. Slip the same stitch back to the left needle (Figure 2), turn the work around and bring the yarn in position for the next stitch, wrapping the slipped stitch with working yarn as you do so. When you come to a wrapped stitch on a subsequent row, hide the wrap by working it together with the wrapped stitch as follows: Insert right needle tip under the wrap (from the front if wrapped stitch is a knit stitch; from the back if wrapped stitch is a purl stitch), then into the stitch on the needle, and work the stitch and its wrap together as a single stitch.

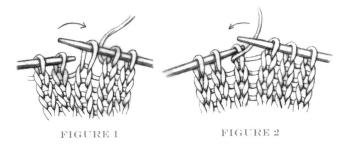

FIGURE 1   FIGURE 2

WEAVING IN ENDS

Once you have blocked your finished pieces, weave in all loose ends. Using a tapestry needle, weave each loose end through about five stitches on the wrong side of the fabric, then pull the end through and trim it close. Do not weave two ends in the same area.

Many knitters find this a very tedious task, but it is well worth putting in the effort. Sew in all ends—don't be tempted to use a long yarn end for sewing up. Use a separate length of yarn to sew pieces together, so that you can undo the seam if necessary without the danger of unraveling your knitting.

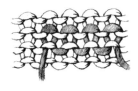

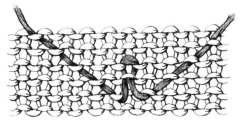

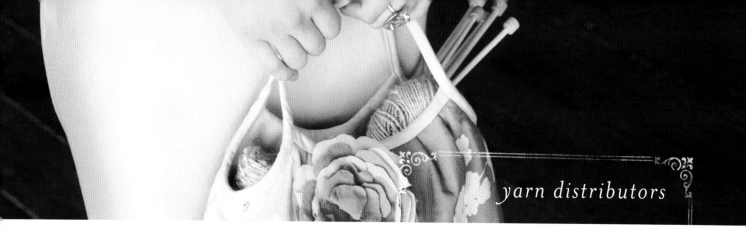

The following companies distribute Louisa Harding
Yarns. Their websites have helpful information regard-
ing yarns, shade cards, and yarn store locations.

UNITED STATES:

Euro Yarns

euroyarns.com

euroyarns@knittingfever.com

(800) 645-3457

Fax (631) 598-5800

CANADA:

Diamond Yarn

diamondyarn.com

diamond@diamondyarn.com

(416) 736-6111

EUROPE:

Designer Yarns Ltd

designeryarns.uk.com

alex@designeryarns.uk.com

(+44 0) 1535 664222

Fax (+44 0) 1535 664333

index

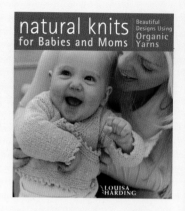